TOP SECRET

Inspiration, Motivation and Encouragement

701 Essential Quotes for Writers

Christopher di Armani

ISBN-13: 978-0987934543
ISBN-10: 0987934546

Published By:

Botanie Valley Productions Inc.
PO Box 507
Lytton, BC V0K 1Z0
http://BotanieValleyProductions.com

Dedication

First and Foremost

This book is dedicated to my sweet and loving wife Lynda.

Without her unwavering support none of this would be possible.

Second

If you live to put words on paper,

If the thought of *not* writing crushes your soul,

If you are happiest pounding on your keyboard at 3am,

This book is dedicated to you.

It doesn't matter what you write.

It matters that you write.

Table of Contents

Foreword

This book is a compilation of 701 quotes covering 39 aspects of writing and the writing life.

No writer learns the craft of writing in a vacuum. We learn our craft by reading, writing and learning from the experience of others. That is the focus of this collection.

Within the pages of this book you will discover quotes to make you laugh, cry and every emotion between. Some will be as familiar as old friends, others you will meet for the first time. They all have a common theme: writers share the same experiences and we learn from each other.

This book is a resource for when you need inspiration or encouragement. It's meant to cheer you up as well as make you think. Above all it's meant to motivate you to write.

From time to time I need a reminder I am not the first writer to sit alone in my writing room happy, sad or somewhere in between. Many a talented writer has sat alone in his or her writing room in joy, despair or something between.

We are not alone. We are never alone. It's important to remember that. Every writer is accompanied by those who wrote before us. They sit on our shoulder, silently watching over us as we create new worlds populated by magical characters.

To paraphrase something said to me long ago in another line of work:

> *"However elated I am about today's writing, tomorrow is another day. However soul-crushing today's writing was, tomorrow is another day."*

I hope this compilation will encourage you in your writing journey.

Most of all I hope this collection encourages you as you write great stories.

A Request for Writing Quotes

If you have a favourite quote and you don't see it in this book please send it to me using the page below.

I am working on a second book of quotes for writers and I would love to include your favourites in that compilation.

http://ChristopherDiArmani.net/Writing-Quote-Submission

Chapter 1 – On Advice to Writers

"Keep a notebook. Travel with it, eat with it, sleep with it. Slap into it every stray thought that flutters up into your brain. Cheap paper is less perishable than gray matter, and lead pencil markings endure longer than memory."

— Jack London

****

"Be ruthless about protecting writing days, i.e. do not cave in to endless requests to have 'essential' and 'long overdue' meetings on those days."

— J.K. Rowling

****

"To be a writer – write! To be an author – publish! To be a bestselling author – never stop writing!"

— David Maxwell

****

"No one can write decently who is distrustful of the reader's intelligence or whose attitude is patronizing."

— E. B. White

****

"For a creative writer, possession of the 'truth' is less important than emotional sincerity."

— George Orwell

****

"Aspiring authors, get this through your head. Cover art serves one purpose, and one purpose only, to get potential customers interested long enough to pick up the book to read the back cover blurb. In the internet age that means the thumbnail image needs to be interesting enough to click on. That's what covers are for."

— Larry Correia

****

"Talent does what it can; genius does what it must."

—Edward G. Bulwer-Lytton

****

"No tears in the writer,
No tears in the reader.
No surprise for the writer,
No surprise for the reader."

— Robert Frost

****

"Don't use words too big for the subject. Don't say 'infinitely' when you mean 'very;' otherwise you'll have no word left when you want to talk about something really infinite."

— C.S. Lewis

****

"Close the door. Write with no one looking over your shoulder. Don't try to figure out what other people want to hear from you; figure out what you have to say. It's the one and only thing you have to offer."

— Barbara Kingsolver

****

"All you have to do is write one true sentence. Write the truest sentence that you know."

— Ernest Hemingway

******

"Write what should not be forgotten."

— Isabel Allende

******

"Heinlein's Rules for Writers:

Rule 1: You Must Write.
Rule 2: Finish What Your Start.
Rule 3: You Must Refrain From Rewriting, Except to Editorial Order.
Rule 4: You Must Put Your Story on the Market.
Rule 5: You Must Keep it on the Market until it has Sold."

— Robert A. Heinlein

******

"Maugham then offers the greatest advice anyone could give to a young author: 'At the end of an interrogation sentence, place a question mark. You'd be surprised how effective it can be.'"

Woody Allen

******

"There are two moments worthwhile in writing, the one when you start and the other when you throw it in the waste-paper basket."

— Samuel Beckett

******

"It's been my experience that most writers don't talk about their craft – they just do it."

— Alfred Lansing

****

"Giving a reader a sex scene that is only half right is like giving her half a kitten. It is not half as cute as a whole kitten; it is a bloody, god-awful mess. A half-good sex scene is not half as hot; it actually moves into negative numbers, draining any heat from the surrounding material."

— Sandra Newman

****

"I would advise anyone who aspires to a writing career that before developing his talent he would be wise to develop a thick hide."

— Harper Lee

****

"There are three rules for writing a novel. Unfortunately no one knows what they are."

— W. Somerset Maugham

****

"They're fancy talkers about themselves, writers. If I had to give young writers advice, I would say don't listen to writers talking about writing or themselves."

—Lillian Hellman

****

"A person is a fool to become a writer. His only compensation is absolute freedom. He has no master except his own soul and that, I am sure, is why he does it."

— Roald Dahl

****

"Write a short story every week. It's not possible to write 52 bad stories in a row."

— Ray Bradbury

****

"Artists don't talk about art. Artists talk about work. If I have anything to say to you writers, it's stop thinking of writing as art. Think of it as work."

— Paddy Chayefsky

****

"No man who bothers about originality will ever be original: whereas if you simply try to tell the truth (without caring twopence how often it has been told before) you will, nine times out of ten, become original without ever having noticed it."

— C.S. Lewis

****

"The great work must inevitably be obscure, except to the very few, to those who like the author himself are initiated into the mysteries. Communication then is secondary: it is perpetuation which is important. For this only one good reader is necessary."

— Henry Miller

Chapter 2 – On Being a Writer

"I am a writer. Therefore I am not sane."

— Edgar Allan Poe

******

"If you wish to be a writer, write."

— Epictetus

******

"There is nothing to writing. All you do is sit down at a typewriter and bleed."

— Ernest Hemingway

******

"A writer is someone for whom writing is more difficult than it is for other people."

— Thomas Mann

******

"Writing is not necessarily something to be ashamed of, but do it in private and wash your hands afterwards."

— Robert A. Heinlein

******

"The only way to do great work is to love what you do."

— Steve Jobs

******

"The only thing I was fit for was to be a writer, and this notion rested solely on my suspicion that I would never be fit for real work, and that writing didn't require any."

— Russell Baker

****

"The great advantage of being a writer is that you can spy on people. You're there, listening to every word, but part of you is observing. Everything is useful to a writer, you see – every scrap, even the longest and most boring of luncheon parties."

— Graham Greene

****

"Write what you know. Write what you want to know more about. Write what you're afraid to write about."

— Cec Murphy

****

"There is no 'writer's lifestyle.' All that matters is what you leave on the page."

— Zadie Smith

****

"Quiet people have the loudest minds."

— Stephen King

****

"I'm writing novels because I found something I love because I tried it. Don't be afraid to shake it up."

— Adriana Trigani

****

"The reason that fiction is more interesting than any other form of literature, to those who really like to study people, is that in fiction the author can really tell the truth without humiliating himself."

— Eleanor Roosevelt

****

"We are all apprentices in a craft where no one ever becomes a master."

— Ernest Hemingway

****

"If you truly are going to be a writer, there must be somewhere within you the drive, the desire, to put pen to paper, fingers to keyboard, and actually write."

— Kaye Dacus

****

"Half of what I write is garbage but if I don't write it down it decomposes in my head."

— Jarod Kintz

****

"Writer's aren't people exactly. Or, if they're any good, they're a whole lot of people trying so hard to be one person."

— F. Scott Fitzgerald

****

"No one connected intimately with a writer has any appreciation of his temperament, except to think him overdoing everything."

— Zane Grey

****

"If you have any young friends who aspire to become writers, the second greatest favor you can do them is to present them with copies of The Elements of Style. The first greatest, of course, is to shoot them now while they're happy."

— Dorothy Parker

****

"Love the work: the grind, the dreaming, the distracted not-sleep, all of it. It's the one thing in the job that will always be there, and the real pleasure in the profession. Everything else is luck."

— Glen Hirshberg

****

"The secret of being a writer: not to expect others to value what you've done as you value it, not to expect anyone else to perceive in it the emotions you have. Once this is understood all will be well."

— Joyce Carol Oates

****

"The mind of a writer can be a truly terrifying thing. Isolated, neurotic, caffeine-addled, crippled by procrastination, consumed by feelings of panic, self-loathing, and soul-crushing inadequacy. And that's on a good day."

— Robert De Niro

****

"God, Himself, wrote the 10 Commandments into stone with his own finger. He told the epic of mankind, our origins and our future, in a book. For me, there is no more noble a cause and no more honorable a vocation than to say, like Him, I am a writer."

— Gerard de Marigny

****

"There is no greater agony than bearing an untold story inside you."

— Maya Angelou

****

"I wanted to be a politician and a movie star. But I was born a writer. If you're born that, you can't change it. You're going to do it whether you want to or not."

— Gore Vidal

****

"Five common traits of good writers:

(1) They have something to say.

(2) They read widely and have done so since childhood.

(3) They possess what Isaac Asimov calls a 'capacity for clear thought,' able to go from point to point in an orderly sequence, an A to Z approach.

(4) They're geniuses at putting their emotions into words.

(5) They possess an insatiable curiosity, constantly asking Why and How."

— James J. Kilpatrick

****

"The true alchemists do not change lead into gold; they change the world into words."

— William H. Gass

Chapter 3 – On Changing the World

"Writing is a dangerous profession. There is no telling what hole you may rip in society's carefully woven master narrative."

— Danielle Orner

******

"It is the writer who might catch the imagination of young people, and plant a seed that will flower and come to fruition."

— Isaac Asimov

******

"Creative writers are always greater than the causes that they represent."

— E. M. Forster

******

"If people cannot write well, they cannot think well, and if they cannot think well, others will do their thinking for them."

— George Orwell

******

"What one writer can make in the solitude of one room is something no power can easily destroy."

— Salman Rushdie

******

"There is a ruthlessness to the creative act. It often involves a betrayal of the status quo."

— Alan Watt

******

"Hypocrisy is our friend. Power structures have to pretend to hold values in order to win the loyalty of at least some of society. We can use the gap between those professed values and reality to move people to try to change the reality towards the values."

— Justin Podur

****

"To write well about the elegant world you have to know it and experience it to the depths of your being… what matters is not whether you love it or hate it, but only to be quite clear about your position regarding it."

— Italo Calvino

****

"Writers do not merely reflect and interpret life, they inform and shape life."

— E.B. White

****

"Write something that's worth fighting over. Because that's how you change things. That's how you create art."

— Jeff Goins

****

Chapter 4 – On Characters

"First, find out what your hero wants, then just follow him!"

— Ray Bradbury

****

"It begins with a character, usually, and once he stands up on his feet and begins to move, all I can do is trot along behind him with a paper and pencil trying to keep up long enough to put down what he says and does."

— William Faulkner

****

"The best way to reveal a character is to get them to open their mouth."

— Roddy Doyle

****

"You can't blame the writer for what the characters say."

— Truman Capote

****

"Don't let yourself slip and get any perfect characters... keep them people, people, people, and don't let them get to be symbols."

— Ernest Hemingway

****

"The character that lasts is an ordinary guy with some extraordinary qualities."

— Raymond Chandler

****

"Each writer is born with a repertory company in his head. Shakespeare had perhaps 20 players. I have 10 or so, and that's a lot. As you get older, you become more skillful at casting them."

— Gore Vidal

****

"When writing a novel a writer should create living people; people not characters. A character is a caricature."

— Ernest Hemingway

****

"If I tell you my character has gray hair, you will not see her. If I tell you she has a tiny scar at the upper left corner of her lip from which protrudes one gray whisker you will make up the rest of her face with absolute clarity. If I tell you my character is waiting in the car, you won't be 'caught,' but if I tell you he pushes his fingers down from in the crack of the car seat where the ancient leather has pulled away from the seat frame, and pulls up a small coin purse with a faded note in it, you will be mine."

— Pat Schneider

****

"I try to create characters that I am fascinated by or on some level intrigued by or can't stand."

— Terry McMullan

****

"Every search for a hero must begin with something which every hero requires – a villain."

— Jurgen Muller

****

"Be sure not to discuss your hero's state of mind. Make it clear from his actions."

— Anton Chekhov

****

"The core of every good story is a character for whom we care, and not just care a little but care deeply. This alone is no easy task: such a character must be likable, but not annoying. He must have virtues but remain imperfect. She must possess the potential for sacrifice, for selflessness, for selfishness, for evil. He may be funny but not only that. She may be serious not not only that. He comprises so many dimensions but not so many that he seems unreal or un-pin-downable."

— Chuck Wendig

****

"You don't really understand an antagonist until you understand why he's a protagonist in his own version of the world."

— John Rogers

****

"If you're struggling with writing a character, write 20 things that the reader will never know about your character. These will naturally bleed into your writing and provide a richness even though you don't share the detail."

— Barbara Poelle

****

"Treat all your secondary characters like they think the book is about them."

— Jocelyn Hughes

****

"A villain is just a victim whose story hasn't been told."

— Chris Colfer

****

"Kill your darlings, kill your darlings, even when it breaks your egocentric little scribbler's heart, kill your darlings."

— Stephen King

****

"Remember that you don't write a story because you have an idea but because you have a believable character."

— Flannery O'Connor

****

"I will go to my grave in a state of abject endless fascination that we all have the capacity to become emotionally involved with a personality that doesn't exist."

— Berkeley Breathed

****

"You take people, you put them on a journey, you give them peril, you find out who they really are."

— Joss Whedon

****

"I always tell my writing students that every good piece of writing begins with both a mystery and a love story. And that every single sentence must be a poem. And that economy is the key to all good writing. And that every character has to have a secret."

— Silas House

****

Chapter 5 – On Creativity

"Creativity is an act of defiance."

— Twyla Tharp

****

"If you have built castles in the air, your work need not be lost; that is where they should be."

—Henry David Thoreau

****

"First you jump off the cliff and you build your wings on the way down."

— Ray Bradbury

****

"You can't use up creativity. The more you use, the more you have."

— Maya Angelou

****

"In both writing and sleeping, we learn to be physically still at the same time we are encouraging our minds to unlock from the humdrum rational thinking of our daytime lives."

— Stephen King

****

"When in doubt, have a man come through the door with a gun in his hand."

— Raymond Chandler

****

"Let your story grow. Let it surprise you, and it will certainly surprise your readers."

— M. Kirin

****

"Somebody said that writers are like otters… Otters, if they do a trick and you give them a fish, the next time they'll do a better trick or a different trick because they'd already done that one. And writers tend to be otters. Most of us get pretty bored doing the same trick. We've done it, so let's do something different."

—Neil Gaiman

****

"The only way of finding the limits of the possible is by going beyond them into the impossible."

—Arthur C. Clarke

****

"People on the outside think there's something magical about writing, that you go up in the attic at midnight and cast the bones and come down in the morning with a story, but it isn't like that. You sit in back of the typewriter and you work, and that's all there is to it."

— Harlan Ellison

****

"My ideas usually come not at my desk writing but in the midst of living."

— Anais Nin

****

"Be obscure clearly."

— E.B. White

******

"Stories of imagination tend to upset those without one."

— Terry Pratchett

******

"Cheat your landlord if you can and must, but do not try to shortchange the Muse. It cannot be done. You can't fake quality any more than you can fake a good meal."

—William S. Burroughs

******

"The best time for planning a book is while you're doing the dishes."

— Agatha Christie

******

"The role of a writer is not to say what we all can say, but what we are unable to say."

— Anais Nin

******

"Don't think. Thinking is the enemy of creativity. It's self-conscious and anything self-conscious is lousy. You can't 'try' to do things. You simply 'must' do things."

— Ray Bradbury

******

"The chief enemy of creativity is good sense."

— Pablo Picasso

****

"Your intuition knows what to write, so get out of the way."

— Ray Bradbury

****

"Imagination? It is the one thing beside honesty that a good writer must have. The more he learns from experience the more he can imagine."

— Ernest Hemingway

****

"Try any goddamn thing you like, no matter how boringly normal or outrageous. If it works, fine. If it doesn't, toss it. Toss it even if you love it."

— Stephen King

****

"Talented writing makes things happen in the reader's mind – vividly, forcefully – that good writing, which stops with clarity and logic, doesn't."

— Samuel Delany

****

"In any art you're allowed to steal anything if you can make it better."

— Ernest Hemingway

****

"Write what disturbs you, what you fear, what you have not been willing to speak about. Be willing to be split open."

— Natalie Goldberg

****

"What people are ashamed of usually makes for a good story."

— F. Scott Fitzgerald

****

"Imagination is the only weapon in the war against reality."

— Lewis Carroll

****

"Always dream and shoot higher than you know you can do…Try to be better than yourself."

— John Steinbeck

****

"I didn't set out to write this book. It crept up on me when I wasn't looking, when I didn't know I was writing it."

— Mark David Gerson

****

"I am like a little pencil in God's hand. He does the writing. The pencil has nothing to do with it."

— Mother Teresa

****

Free Writing Timer for Authors

I do not believe in writer's block. I do, however, believe in writer's procrastination.

It's an affliction I suffer from each and every day. It's a plague on my productivity, as I am sure it is on yours.

One of the tools in my arsenal to combat procrastination is my Writing Timer. It's a simple little program (Windows only) that allows me to set an amount of time where I do nothing but write.

Of course I wrote the program as part of my own procrastination from writing. Ironic, right?

The concept is simple. Open the timer. Set it for 5, 10, 15, 20 or 30 minutes.

Click Start. Then write.

It doesn't matter what you write. Just write like you're possessed by demons. Or chased by them. Whatever works.

Whenever you know you ought to be writing but are doing everything *except* writing, admit defeat at the hands of writer's procrastination and start the timer.

Then write.

It just works.

To get your free copy of my writing timer just visit the link below.

http://christopherdiarmani.net/Free-Writing-Timer

****

Chapter 6 – On Criticism

"Some who have read the book, or at any rate have reviewed it, have found it boring, absurd, or contemptible, and I have no cause to complain, since I have similar opinions of their works, or of the kinds of writing that they evidently prefer."

— J.R.R Tolkien

****

"If you show someone something you've written, you give them a sharpened stake, lie down in your coffin, and say, 'When you're ready'."

— David Mitchell

****

"To avoid criticism say nothing, do nothing, be nothing."

— Aristotle

****

"Don't pay any attention to what they write about you. Just measure it in inches."

— Andy Warhol

****

"Let me never fall into the vulgar mistake of dreaming that I am persecuted whenever I am contradicted."

— Ralph Waldo Emerson

****

"He who dares not offend cannot be honest."

— Thomas Paine

****

"Do what you feel in your heart to be right – for you'll be criticized anyway."

— Eleanor Roosevelt

****

"Ignore all hatred and criticism. Live for what you create, and die protecting it."

— Lady Gaga

****

"You have enemies? Good. That means you've stood up for something, sometime in your life."

— Winston Churchill

****

"Remember: when people tell you something's wrong or doesn't work for them, they are almost always right. When they tell you exactly what they think is wrong and how to fix it, they are almost always wrong."

— Neil Gaiman

****

"The writer of originality, unless dead, is always shocking, scandalous; novelty disturbs and repels."

— Simone de Beauvoir

****

"Never argue with stupid people. They will drag you down to their level and then beat you with experience."

— Mark Twain

****

"Whatever course you decide upon, there is always someone to tell you that you are wrong. There are always difficulties arising that tempt you to believe your critics are right. To map out a course of action and follow it to an end requires some of the same courage that a soldier needs. Peace has its victories, but it takes brave men and women to win them."

— Ralph Waldo Emerson

****

"The artist doesn't have time to listen to the critics. The ones who want to be writers read the reviews, the ones who want to write don't have the time to read reviews."

— William Faulkner

****

"If critics say your work stinks it's because they want it to stink and they can make it stink by scaring you into conformity with their comfortable little standards. Standards so low that they can no longer be considered 'dangerous' but set in place in their compartmental understandings."

— Jack Kerouac

****

"Writers are dangerous people. Never take a writer for granted. They are snipers armed with words. They know how to aim with sentences, how to fire with paragraphs, and how to immortalize their kills in verse."

— Nikita Gill

****

"If you are afraid of the critics you will never write a word."

— Bangambiki Habyarimana

****

"To acquire true self power you have to feel beneath no one, be immune to criticism and be fearless."

— Deepak Chopra

****

"I would rather be attacked than unnoticed. For the worst thing you can do to an author is to be silent as to his works."

— Samuel Johnson

****

"The public is wonderfully tolerant. It forgives everything except genius."

— Oscar Wilde

****

"Lie naked on the table, and let them cut. Criticism is surgery, and humility is the anesthetic that allows you to tolerate it. In the end, the process will make you a stronger, more flexible, and truly creative writer. It will replace attitude with genuine confidence, and empty arrogance with artistry."

— Molly Cochran

****

"These critics who crucify me do not guess the littlest part of my sincerity. They must be burned in a blaze. I cannot learn from them."

— Zane Grey

****

Chapter 7 – On Deadlines

"I love deadlines. I like the whooshing sound they make as they fly by."

— Douglas Adams

****

"If my doctor told me I had only six minutes to live I wouldn't brood. I'd type a little faster."

— Isaac Asimov

****

"Deadlines just aren't real to me until I'm staring one in the face."

— Rick Riordan

****

"A deadline is negative inspiration. Still, it's better than no inspiration at all."

— Rita Mae Brown

****

"Goals are dreams with deadlines."

— Diana Scharf

****

"I am a person who works well under pressure. In fact, I work so well under pressure that at times, I will procrastinate in order to create this pressure."

— Stephanie Pearl-McPhee

****

"Are you aware that rushing toward a goal is a sublimated death wish? It's no coincidence we call them 'deadlines.'"

— Tom Robbins

******

"A deadline is a finish line. Don't stop 'til the door shuts in your face!"

— Raven Moore

******

"...a deadline should not prevent you from writing, but writing will help prevent you from missing your deadline. Then write a word. Then remind yourself of that again. And then write another and hey, look at you! You're spitting in that deadline's eye."

— Courtney Summers

******

"A hammer made of deadlines is the surest tool for crushing writer's block."

— Ryan Lilly

******

"If the novels are still being read in 50 years, no one is ever going to say: 'What's great about that sixth book is that he met his deadline!' It will be about how the whole thing stands up."

— George R.R. Martin

******

"I don't need time, I need a deadline."

— Duke Ellington

******

"A deadline is, simply put, optimism in its most kick-ass form. It's a potent force that, when wielded with respect, will level any obstacle in it's path. This is especially true when it comes to creative pursuits."

— Chris Baty

****

"When you are a free and independent writer, without employer, without hours or deadlines, you have to play little games to force yourself into the actual writing. For me, one game is to announce...that I have finally decided on my next book, that I am ready to write it...to put my pride on the line."

— Irving Wallace

****

"Journalist: a person without any ideas but with an ability to express them; a writer whose skill is improved by a deadline: the more time he has, the worse he writes."

— Karl Kraus

****

"At times, it is better to 'just do it' than to 'do it right.' One reason New Year resolutions don't work is because we expect too much from ourselves. Rush, meet your deadlines, you can always continue from where you stopped next year."

— Asuni LadyZeal

****

"There's nothing an artist needs more – even more than excellent tools and stamina – than a deadline."

— Adriana Trigiani

****

Christopher di Armani

"You know, I always was an early morning or late night writer. Early morning was my favorite; late night was because you had a deadline. And at four in the morning you make up some of your most absurd jokes."

— Joss Whedon

****

"I'm convinced that fear is at the root of most bad writing. If one is writing for one's own pleasure, that fear may be mild – timidity is the word I've used here. If, however, one is working under deadline – a school paper, a newspaper article, the SAT writing sample – that fear may be intense."

— Stephen King

****

"Being proud of my work and wanting to nurture this relationship, I never failed in my commitments to her. In general, I make a point of meeting all my deadlines. But, I distinctly remember one time that I couldn't deliver the job in time…"

— Ajit Kumar Jha

****

"A year from now you may wish you had started today."

— Karen Lamb

****

"The only thing standing between you and your goal is the bullshit story you keep telling yourself as to why you can't achieve it."

— Jordan Belfort

****

Chapter 8 – On Discipline

"The way to write a book is to actually write a book. A pen is useful. Typing is also good. Keep putting words on the page."

— Anne Enright

******

"It's always too soon to quit!"

— Norman Vincent Peale

******

"It's not what we do once in a while that shapes our lives. It's what we do consistently."

— Anthony Robbins

******

"Just set one day's work in front of the last day's work. That's the way it comes out. And that's the only way it does."

— John Steinbeck

******

"I'm writing. The pages are starting to stack up. My morale is improving the more I feel like a writer."

— Neil Gaiman

******

"Be prepared to work hard to be a writer."

— Sandra Brown

******

"Success is a little like wrestling a gorilla. You don't quit when you're tired. You quit when the gorilla is tired."

— Robert Strauss

****

"There is a great deal that either has to be given up or be taken away from you if you are going to succeed in writing a body of work."

— Susan Sontag

****

"Work on one thing at a time until finished."

— Henry Miller

****

"The man who moves a mountain begins by carrying away small stones."

— Confucius

****

"Any man who keeps working is not a failure. He may not be a great writer, but if he applies the old-fashioned virtues of hard, constant labor, he'll eventually make some kind of career for himself as writer."

— Ray Bradbury

****

"You never know what's around the corner. It could be everything. Or it could be nothing. You keep putting one foot in front of the other, and then one day you look back and you've climbed a mountain."

— Tom Hiddleston

****

"What's the bravest thing you ever did?"

He spat in the road a bloody phlegm.

"Getting up this morning."

— Cormac McCarthy

****

"When I'm writing I know I'm doing the thing I was born to do."

— Anne Sexton

****

"Writing a book is always hard work. It's much easier to think of new ideas. You'll get to the middle of the manuscript and you'll think 'Oh, this is too hard. I think I'll start another book instead and that will be easier.' DON'T! That new book won't be any easier."

— Rick Riordan

****

"Serious writers write, inspired or not. Over time they discover that routine is a better friend than inspiration."

— Ralph Keyes

****

"You need a certain amount of nerve to be a writer."

— Margaret Atwood

****

"The difficulty, the ordeal, is to start."

— Zane Grey

****

"The Secret to Writing a Bestseller:

You write.

You stop dreaming of writing.

You stop talking about writing.

You stop wishing you were writing.

And you write."

— Jonathan Gunson

****

"You need three things to become a successful novelist: talent, luck and discipline. Discipline is the one element of those three things that you can control, and so that is the one that you have to focus on controlling, and you just have to hope and trust in the other two."

— Michael Chabon

****

"Don't over edit. Don't second-guess yourself, or your ideas. Just write. Write every day, and keep at it. Don't get discouraged with the rejections. Tape them up on your office wall, to remind you of all the hard work you put in when you finally start getting published! It's all about persistence and passion. And have fun with it. Don't forget to have fun."

— Heather Grace Stewart

****

Chapter 9 – On Editing

"If it sounds like writing, I rewrite it. Or, if proper usage gets in the way, it may have to go. I can't allow what we learned in English composition to disrupt the sound and rhythm of the narrative."

—Elmore Leonard

****

"The time to begin writing an article is when you have finished it to your satisfaction. By that time you begin to clearly and logically perceive what it is you really want to say."

— Mark Twain

****

"Not that the story need be long, but it will take a long while to make it short."

— Henry David Thoreau

****

"My own experience is that once a story has been written, one has to cross out the beginning and the end. It is there that we authors do most of our lying."

— Anton Chekhov

****

"I can't write five words but that I change seven."

— Dorothy Parker

****

"Write your first draft with your heart. Rewrite with your head."

— Mike Rich

****

"The research is the easiest. The outline is the most fun. The first draft is the hardest, because every word of the outline has to be fleshed out. The rewrite is very satisfying."

— Ken Follett

****

"Fiction does not spring into the world fully grown, like Athena. It is the process of writing and rewriting that makes a fiction original, if not profound."

— John Gardner

****

"Revision is one of the true pleasures of writing. I love the flowers of afterthought."

— Bernard Malamud

****

"It is perfectly okay to write garbage – as long as you edit brilliantly."

— C. J. Cherryh

****

"I try to leave out the parts that people skip."

— Elmore Leonard

****

"The difference between the almost right word and the right word is really a large matter – it's the difference between the lightning bug and the lightning."

— Mark Twain

****

"If something isn't working, if you have a story that you've built and it's blocked and you can't figure it out, take your favourite scene, or your very best idea or set-piece, and cut it. It's brutal but sometimes inevitable."

— Joss Whedon

****

"So the writer who breeds more words than he needs, is making a chore for the reader who reads."

— Dr. Seuss

****

"Writing is like riding a bike. Once you gain momentum, the hills are easier. Editing, however, requires a motor and some horsepower."

— Gina McKnight

****

"Writing is rewriting. Even after you've gotten an agent and an editor, you'll have to rewrite. If you fall in love with the vision you want for your work and not your words, the rewriting will become easier."

— Nora DeLoach

****

"Some editors are failed writers, but so are most writers."

— T. S. Eliot

****

"A really well-done first draft of a book bares your soul. The purpose of revision is so that everyone who reads the published version believes you were writing about theirs."

— James A. Owen

****

"Look for the clutter in your writing and prune it ruthlessly. Be grateful for everything you can throw away. Reexamine each sentence you put on paper. Is every word doing new work? Can any thought be expressed with more economy? Is anything pompous or pretentious or faddish? Are you hanging on to something useless just because you think it's beautiful? Simplify, simplify."

— William Zinsser

****

Chapter 10 – On Encouragement

"I know it's difficult in the beginning. But, listen. If you have the impulse to write, do yourself a favor, do the world a favor, and write."

— Christy Hall

****

"It's none of their business that you have to learn to write. Let them think you were born that way."

— Ernest Hemingway

****

"Be an Encourager. When you encourage others, you boost their self-esteem, enhance their self-confidence, make them work harder, lift their spirits and make them successful in their endeavors. Encouragement goes straight to the heart and is always available. Be an encourager. Always."

— Roy T. Bennett

****

"And what, you ask, does writing teach us? First and foremost, it reminds us that we are alive and it is a gift and a privilege, not a right."

— Ray Bradbury

****

"If you're a writer, your first duty, a duty you owe to yourself and your readers, and to your writing itself, is to become wonderful. To become the best writer you can possibly be."

— Theodora Goss

****

"Start telling the stories that only you can tell, because there'll always be better writers than you and there'll always be smarter writers than you. There will always be people who are much better at doing this or doing that – but you are the only you.

Tarantino – you can criticize everything that Quentin does – but nobody writes Tarantino stuff like Tarantino. He is the best Tarantino writer there is, and that was actually the thing that people responded to – they're going 'this is an individual writing with his own point of view.'

There are better writers than me out there, there are smarter writers, there are people who can plot better – there are all those kinds of things, but there's nobody who can write a Neil Gaiman story like I can."

— Neil Gaiman

******

"I can shake off everything as I write. My sorrows disappear, my courage is reborn."

— Anne Frank

******

Chapter 11 – On Experience

"It took me fifteen years to discover I had no talent for writing, but I couldn't give it up because by that time I was too famous."

— Robert Benchley

****

"The unread story is not a story; it is little black marks on wood pulp. The reader, reading it, makes it live: a live thing, a story."

— Ursula K. Le Guin

****

"The original writer is not one who imitates nobody, but one whom nobody can imitate."

— Chateaubriand

****

"We [writers] must know that we can never escape the common misery and that our only justification, if indeed there is a justification, is to speak up, insofar as we can, for those who cannot do so."

— Albert Camus

****

"The ear is the only true writer and the only true reader."

— Robert Frost

****

"You must stay drunk on writing so reality cannot destroy you."

— Ray Bradbury

****

"I know I was writing stories when I was five. I don't know what I did before that. Just loafed, I suppose."

— P.G. Wodehouse

****

"For a person whose sole burning ambition is to write – like myself – college is useless beyond the Sophomore year."

— William Styron

****

"What nobody tells you is that spending an entire day being paid to do something you love is sometimes a lot less fun than spending an entire day doing something you love for free."

— Allison K. Williams

****

Chapter 12 – On Fear

"The scariest moment is always just before you start."

— Stephen King

****

"If you want to write, you can. Fear stops most people from writing, not lack of talent, whatever that is. Who am I? What right have I to speak? Who will listen to me if I do? You're a human being, with a unique story to tell, and you have every right. If you speak with passion, many of us will listen. We need stories to live, all of us. We live by story. Yours enlarges the circle."

— Richard Rhodes

****

"Be courageous and try to write in a way that scares you a little."

— Holley Gerth

****

"Writing is hard for every last one of us… Coal mining is harder. Do you think miners stand around all day talking about how hard it is to mine for coal? They do not. They simply dig."

— Cheryl Strayed

****

"I think it's fairly common for writers to be afflicted with two simultaneous yet contradictory delusions – the burning certainty that we're unique geniuses and the constant fear that we're witless frauds who are speeding toward epic failure."

— Scott Lynch

****

"Everything you want is on the other side of fear."

— Jack Canfield

****

"What we fear doing most is usually what we most need to do."

— Tim Ferris

****

"Nothing haunts us like the things we don't say."

— Mitch Albom

****

"Too many of us are not living our dreams because we are living our fears."

— Les Brown

****

Chapter 13 – On Finishing

"Finishing a book is just like you took a child out in the back yard and shot it."

— Truman Capote

****

"It's a feeling of happiness that knocks me clean out of adjectives. I think sometimes that the best reason for writing novels is to experience those four and a half hours after you write the final word."

— Zadie Smith

****

"I went for years not finishing anything. Because, of course, when you finish something you can be judged."

— Erica Jong

****

"Great is the art of beginning, but greater is the art of ending."

— Henry Wadsworth Longfellow

****

"Whatever it takes to finish things, finish. You will learn more from a glorious failure than you ever will from something you never finished."

— Neil Gaiman

****

"The hard part about about writing a novel is finishing it."

— Ernest Hemmingway

****

"Writing is hard. That's why so few people stick to it and actually finish things. And why you have a right to be immensely proud when you finish something."

— Andy Ihnatko

****

"I've come to the end of another book alive. At times like this I'm always at a loss for words."

— Joe Coomer

****

"Writers often torture themselves trying to get the words right. Sometimes you must lower your expectations and just finish it."

— Don Roff

****

"You need two things to write a great book: imagination and inclination. Without one, your book will be boring; without the other, your book won't get finished at all."

— Ellie Firestone

****

"Abandon the idea that you are ever going to finish. Lose track of the 400 pages and write just one page for each day. It helps. Then when it gets finished you are always surprised."

— John Steinbeck

****

Chapter 14 – On Finding Your Audience

"If the book is true, it will find an audience that is meant to read it."

— Wally Lamb

****

"People do not deserve to have good writing, they are so pleased with bad."

— Ralph Waldo Emerson

****

"I don't care if a reader hates one of my stories, just as long as he finishes the book."

— Roald Dahl

****

"If you hide your ignorance no one will hit you and you'll never learn."

— Ray Bradbury

****

"Be yourself and your readers will follow you anywhere. Try to commit an act of writing and they will jump overboard to get away."

— William Zinsser

****

"...and above all, you should not think of writing as a way of earning your living. If you do, your work will smell of your poverty. It will be colored by your weakness and be as thin as your hunger. There are other trades which you can take up: make boots, not books."

— Marquis de Sade

****

"I've put in so many enigmas and puzzles that it will keep the professors busy for centuries arguing over what I meant, and that's the only way of insuring one's immortality."

— James Joyce

Chapter 15 – On First Drafts

"The first draft of anything is shit."

— Ernest Hemingway

******

"Don't get it right, get it written."

— Ally Carter

******

"It is better to write a bad first draft than to write no first draft at all."

— Will Shetterly

******

"If I waited for perfection I would never write a word."

— Margaret Atwood

******

"Get it down. Take chances. It may be bad, but it's the only way you can do anything really good."

— William Faulkner

******

"Write freely and as rapidly as possible and throw the whole thing on paper. Never correct or rewrite until the whole thing is down. Rewrite in process is usually found to be an excuse for not going on. It also interferes with flow and rhythm which can only come from a kind of unconscious association with the material."

— John Steinbeck

******

"Do not wait to strike till the iron is hot; but make it hot by striking."

—William B. Sprague

****

"I must write it all out, at any cost. Writing is thinking. It is more than living, for it is being conscious of living."

— Anne Morrow Lindbergh

****

"Almost all good writing begins with terrible first efforts. You need to start somewhere."

— Anne Lamott

****

"The secret of it all is to write in the gush, the throb, the flood of the moment – to put things down without deliberation – without worrying about their style – without waiting for a fit time or place. I always worked that way. I took the first scrap of paper, the first doorstep, the first desk, and wrote, wrote, wrote… By writing at the instant, the very heartbeat of life is caught."

— Walt Whitman

****

"I'm writing a first draft and reminding myself that I'm simply shoveling sand into a box so that later I can build castles."

— Shannon Hale

****

"It's okay to write crap. Just don't try publishing it while it's still crap."

— S.M. Blooding

****

"Don't look back until you've written an entire draft, just begin each day from the last sentence you wrote the preceding day. This prevents those cringing feelings, and means that you have a substantial body of work before you get down to the real work which is all in ... the edit."

— Will Self

****

"It's okay to write a cliché in a first draft; it sets a marker that you can get far, far away from in the rewrites."

— Stewart Stafford

****

"All writing problems are psychological problems. Blocks usually stem from the fear of being judged. If you imagine the world listening, you'll never write a line. That's why privacy is so important. You should write first drafts as if they will never be shown to anyone."

— Erica Jong

****

"Bad writing precedes good writing. This is an infallible rule, so don't waste time trying to avoid bad writing. That just slows down the process. Anything committed to paper can be changed. The idea is the start, and then go from there."

— Janet Hulstrand

****

"How hard can writing be? After all, most of the words are going to be 'and,' 'the,' and 'I,' and 'it,' and so on, and there's a huge number to choose from, so a lot of the work has been done for you."

— Terry Pratchett

****

"Don't give in to doubt. Never be discouraged if your first draft isn't what you thought it would be. Given skill and a story that compels you, muster your determination and make what's on the page closer to what you have in your mind. The chances are that you'll never make them identical. That's one reason I'm still hitting the keyboard. Obsessed by the secrets of my past, I try to put metaphorical versions of them on the page, but each time, no matter how honest and hard my effort, what's in my mind hasn't been fully expressed, compelling me to keep trying. To paraphrase a passage from John Barth's 'Lost in the Funhouse,' I'll die telling stories to myself in the dark. But there's never enough time. There was never enough time."

— David Morrell

****

"For me and most of the other writers I know, writing is not rapturous. In fact, the only way I can get anything written at all is to write really, really shitty first drafts."

— Anne Lamott

****

"I just give myself permission to suck. I delete about 90 percent of my first drafts … so it doesn't really matter much if on a particular day I write beautiful and brilliant prose that will stick in the minds of my readers forever, because there's a 90 percent chance I'm just gonna delete whatever I write anyway. I find this hugely liberating. I also like to remind myself of something my dad said in [response] to writers' block: 'Coal miners don't get coal miners' block.'"

— John Green

****

"When a solid first draft of an original tale is complete...you feel as if you could do anything."

— Christy Hall

****

Chapter 16 – On Grammar and Punctuation

"Let grammar, punctuation, and spelling into your life! Even the most energetic and wonderful mess has to be turned into sentences."

— Terry Pratchett

****

"A man's grammar, like Caesar's wife, should not only be pure, but above suspicion of impurity."

— Edgar Allan Poe

****

"I don't know the rules of grammar... If you're trying to persuade people to do something, or buy something, it seems to me you should use their language, the language they use every day, the language in which they think. We try to write in the vernacular."

— David Ogilvy

****

"Nouns and verbs are the guts of the language. Beware of covering up with adjectives and adverbs."

— A.B. Guthrie Jr.

****

"Writing is an act of faith, not a trick of grammar."

— E. B. White

****

"If the passage absolutely demands cursing, be moderate. A little of it goes a long way. I've seen beginning writers pepper curse words through sentence after sentence.

'If you don't -blanking- get your -blanking-blank-blank- in to this house this -blanking- minute, I'm going to -blank- your -blank- and nail it to the -blanking- door.'

Two things happen when I read this junk: I get bored and I get angry. I didn't pick up your book to read garbage. If this is as clever as you can be, I don't want to read your prose. In life if you met someone who spoke like this, you'd want to flee. Then why put this stuff on the page?

As near as I can determine, this abomination occurs because a writer is corrupted by the awful -blanking- dialog that movies inflict on us these days. It's also a sign of insecurity. The writer wonders if the dialog is strong enough and decides a lot of -blanking-blank- will do the trick.

Someone might object that this kind of dialog is realistic in certain situations – intense scenes involving policemen or soldiers for example. I can only reply that in my research I spend considerable time with policemen and soldiers. Few of them curse any more than a normal person would. This garbage isn't realistic. It merely draws attention to itself and holds back the story. Use it sparingly."

— David Morrell

****

"Anarchy is as detestable in grammar as it is in society."

— Maurice Druon

****

"Grammar is a piano I play by ear. All I know about grammar is its power."

— Joan Didion

****

"Your grammar is a reflection of your image. Good or bad, you have made an impression. And like all impressions, you are in total control."

— Jeffrey Gitomer

****

"'Correct' spelling, indeed, is one of the arts that are far more esteemed by schoolma'ams than by practical men, neck-deep in the heat and agony of the world."

— H.L. Mencken

****

"The only 'ironclad rules' in writing fiction are the laws of physics and the principles of grammar, and even those can be bent."

— Val Kovalin

****

"Would you convey my compliments to the purist who reads your proofs and tell him or her that I write a sort of broken-down patois which is something like the way a Swiss waiter talks, and that when I split an infinitive, God damn it, I split it so it will stay split, and when I interrupt the velvety smoothness of my more or less literate syntax with a few sudden words of bar-room vernacular, that is done with the eyes wide open and the mind relaxed but attentive."

— Raymond Chandler

****

"Art, whatever form it takes, requires hard work, craftsmanship and creativity. As a writer, I know my grammar, cadence, the music of prose, and the art of the narrative."

— F. Sionil Jose

****

"It is really important that focusing on things such as spelling, punctuation, grammar and handwriting doesn't inhibit the creative flow. When I was at school there was a huge focus on copying and testing and it put me off words and stories for years."

— Michael Morpurgo

****

"There is an underlying rhythm to all text. Sentences crashing fall like the waves of the sea, and work unconsciously on the reader. Punctuation is the music of language. As a conductor can influence the experience of the song by manipulating its rhythm, so can punctuation influence the reading experience, bring out the best (or worst) in a text. By controlling the speed of a text, punctuation dictates how it should be read. A delicate world of punctuation lives just beneath the surface of your work, like a world of microorganisms living in a pond. They are missed by the naked eye, but if you use a microscope you will find they exist, and that the pond is, in fact, teeming with life. This book will teach you to become sensitive to this habitat. The more you do, the greater the likelihood of your crafting a finer work in every respect. Conversely the more you turn a blind eye, the greater the likelihood of your creating a cacophonous text and of your being misread."

— Noah Lukeman

****

"When a thought takes one's breath away, a grammar lesson seems an impertinence."

— Thomas W. Higginson

****

"Substitute 'damn' every time you're inclined to write 'very;' your editor will delete it and the writing will be just as it should be."

— Mark Twain

****

"Cut out all those exclamation marks. An exclamation mark is like laughing at your own joke."

— F. Scott Fitzgerald

****

"If there is method here, it is hard to discern it. Let it be repeated: the use of capitals is a matter not of rules but of taste; but consistency is at least not a mark of bad taste."

— H. W. Fowler

****

"The secret to good writing is to use small words for big ideas, not to use big words for small ideas."

— Oliver Markus

****

"I will not go down to posterity talking bad grammar."

— Benjamin Disraeli

****

"People who cannot distinguish between good and bad language, or who regard the distinction as unimportant, are unlikely to think carefully about anything else."

— B. R. Myers

****

"Do not be surprised when those who ignore the rules of grammar also ignore the law. After all, the law is just so much grammar."

— Robert Brault

****

"Skill alone cannot teach or produce a great short story, which condenses the obsession of the creature; it is a hallucinatory presence manifest from the first sentence to fascinate the reader, to make him lose contact with the dull reality that surrounds him, submerging him in another that is more intense and compelling."

— Julio Cortázar

Chapter 17 – On Inspiration

"You can't wait for inspiration. You have to go after it with a club."

— Jack London

******

"Amateurs sit and wait for inspiration, the rest of us just get up and go to work."

— Stephen King

******

"If you wait for inspiration to write; you're not a writer, you're a waiter."

— Dan Poynter

******

"Everybody walks past a thousand story ideas every day. The good writers are the ones who see five or six of them. Most people don't see any."

— Orson Scott Card

******

"We write to taste life twice, in the moment and in retrospection."

— Anais Nin

******

"If there's a book that you want to read, but it hasn't been written yet, then you must write it."

— Toni Morrison

******

"Writing isn't difficult. Writing well is difficult. What is most difficult is being with the interior experience that manifests as resistance to writing."

— H. Raven Rose

****

"Imagination is everything. It is the preview of life's coming attractions."

— Albert Einstein

****

"I have never started a poem yet whose end I knew. Writing a poem is discovering."

— Robert Frost

****

"You get ideas from daydreaming. You get ideas from being bored. You get ideas all the time. The only difference between writers and other people is we notice when we're doing it."

— Neil Gaiman

****

"Inspiration is wonderful when it happens, but the writer must develop an approach for the rest of the time."

— Leonard Bernstein

****

"The true writer, the born writer, will scribble words on scraps of litter, the back of a bus tickets, on the wall of a cell."

— David Nicholls

****

"Either write something worth reading or do something worth writing."

— Benjamin Franklin

****

"Inspiration is a guest that does not willingly visit the lazy."

— Pyotr Tchaikovsky

****

"I write when I'm inspired, and I see to it that I'm inspired at nine o'clock every morning."

— Peter De Vries

****

"If you want to write, if you want to create, you must be the most sublime fool that God ever turned out and sent rambling. You must write every single day of your life.

You must read dreadful dumb books and glorious books, and let them wrestle in beautiful fights inside your head, vulgar one moment, brilliant the next.

You must lurk in libraries and climb the stacks like ladders to sniff books like perfumes and wear books like hats upon your crazy heads.

I wish you a wrestling match with your Creative Muse that will last a lifetime. I wish craziness and foolishness and madness upon you.

May you live with hysteria, and out of it make fine stories – science fiction or otherwise. Which finally means, may you be in love every day for the next 20,000 days. And out of that love, remake a world."

— Ray Bradbury

****

"Because when I write, it's more than just me at a keyboard. It's the universe converging within the pandemonium of my mind and turning it into something beautiful."

— Lindsey Evenstar

****

"Inspiration comes from your writing. Thoughts meander subliminally through our subconscious, at night when we sleep the brain is working. In the act of writing, phrases come out and you think: wow, did I write this? Did I have that insight? Sometimes you know something is good, good within your own limits, and those parts make life worth living."

— Chloe Thurlow

****

"I have been successful probably because I have always realized that I knew nothing about writing and have merely tried to tell an interesting story entertainingly."

— Edgar Rice Burroughs

****

"Recipe For Greatness – To bear up under loss; To fight the bitterness of defeat and the weakness of grief; To be victor over anger; To smile when tears are close; To resist disease and evil men and base instincts; To hate hate and to love love; To go on when it would seem good to die; To look up with unquenchable faith in something ever more about to be. That is what any man can do, and be great."

— Zane Grey

****

Chapter 18 – On Magic

"A story was a form of telepathy. By means of inking symbols onto a page she was able to send thoughts and feelings from her mind to her reader's. It was a magical process so commonplace that no one stopped to wonder at it."

— Ian McEwan

****

"Writing isn't about making money, getting famous, getting dates, getting laid, or making friends. In the end it's about enriching the lives of those who will read your work, and enriching your own life as well. It's about getting up, getting well, and getting over. Getting happy, okay? Getting happy. ...this book...is a permission slip: you can, you should, and if you're brave enough to start, you will. Writing is magic, as much the water of life as any other creative art. The water is free. So drink. Drink and be filled up."

— Stephen King

****

"If you don't think there is magic in writing, you probably won't write anything magical."

— Terry Brooks

****

"Do they sense it, these dead writers, when their books are read? Does a pinprick of light appear in their darkness? Is their soul stirred by the feather touch of another mind reading theirs? I do hope so."

— Diane Setterfield

****

"The object of storytelling, like the object of magic, is not to explain or to resolve, but rather to create and to perform miracles of the imagination. To extend the boundaries of the mysterious. To push into the unknown in pursuit of still other unknowns. To reach into one's heart, down into that place where the stories are, bringing up the mystery of oneself."

— Tim O'Brien

******

"That's the thing about books. They let you travel without moving your feet."

— Jhumpa Lahiri

******

"Always remember that writing is an alliance between author and reader. With every line we put down on the page, we need to leave room for the reader's imagination and intellect."

— Hal Zina Bennett

******

"Books are uniquely portable magic."

— Stephen King

******

"A book is a dream that you hold in your hand."

— Neil Gaiman

******

Chapter 19 – On Motivation

"A writer is a writer not because she writes well or easily, because she has amazing talent, or because everything she does is golden. A writer is a writer because, even when there is no hope, even when nothing you do shows any sign of promise, you keep writing anyway."

— Junot Diaz

******

"Never write anything that does not give you great pleasure. Emotion is easily transferred from the writer to the reader."

— Joseph Joubert

******

"Those who find ugly meanings in beautiful things are corrupt without being charming. This is a fault. Those who find beautiful meanings in beautiful things are the cultivated. For these there is hope. They are the elect to whom beautiful things mean only Beauty. There is no such thing as a moral or an immoral book. Books are well written, or badly written. That is all."

— Oscar Wilde

******

"A creative man is motivated by the desire to achieve, not by the desire to beat others."

— Ayn Rand

******

"Motivation will almost always beat mere talent."

— Norman Ralph Augustine

****

"If you're going to be a writer you have to be one of the great ones... After all, there are better ways to starve to death."

— Gabriel García Márquez

****

"I write to give myself strength. I write to be the characters that I am not. I write to explore all the things I'm afraid of."

— Joss Whedon

****

"Tomorrow may be hell, but today was a good writing day and on the good writing days nothing else matters."

— Neil Gaiman

****

"I wonder sometimes if the motivation for writers ought to be contempt, not admiration."

— Orson Scott Card

****

"Nothing is impossible. The word itself says 'I'm Possible.'"

— Audrey Hepburn

****

Chapter 20 – On The Night

"I've always loved the night, when everyone else is asleep and the world is all mine. It's quiet and dark – the perfect time for creativity."

— Jonathan Harnisch

****

"3am is the hour of writers, painters, poets, over-thinkers, silent seekers and creative people. We know who you are. We can see your light on."

— Nicole Storey

****

"A writer loves the dark, loves it, but is always fumbling around in the light."

— Joy Williams

****

"You never have to change anything you got up in the middle of the night to write."

— Saul Bellow

****

"If I fall asleep with a pen in my hand, don't remove it. I might be writing in my dreams."

— Terry Guillemets

****

"Writing is my obsession, my passion. My relationship with it is one of the most complex and agonizing and richly vexing that I have in my life."

— Julianna Baggott

Chapter 21 – On Obsession

"Real writers are those who want to write, need to write, have to write."

— Robert Penn Warren

****

"Writers are desperate people and when they stop being desperate they stop being writers."

— Charles Bukowski

****

"I write because I can't not write. If I have an idea circling in my brain and I can't get it out, it begins to poison my waking existence, until I'm unable to function in polite company or even hold a simple conversation."

— Jodi Picoult

****

"Had I been blessed with even limited access to my own mind there would have been no reason to write."

— Joan Didion

****

"Writing is a calling, not a choice."

— Isabelle Allende

****

"To survive, you must tell stories."

— Umberto Eco

****

"Writing a book is a horrible, exhausting struggle, like a long bout of some painful illness. One would never undertake such a thing if one were not driven on by some demon whom one can neither resist nor understand. For all one knows that demon is simply the same instinct that makes a baby squall for attention. And yet it is also true that one can write nothing readable unless one constantly struggles to efface one's own personality. Good prose is like a windowpane."

— George Orwell

****

"A non-writing writer is a monster courting insanity."

— Franz Kafka

****

"It is impossible to discourage the real writers. They don't give a damn what you say, they're going to write."

— Sinclair Lewis

****

"You don't write because you want to say something. You write because you have something to say."

— F. Scott Fitzgerald

****

"The trade of authorship is a violent and indestructible obsession."

— George Sand

****

"A writer will always be a writer. It's not a choice, it's a destiny."

— Stephanie Lennox

****

"Writing has to be an obsession – it's only for those who say, 'I'm not going to do anything else.'"

— Lorrie Moore

****

"What moves those of genius, what inspires their work is not new ideas, but their obsession with the idea that what has already been said is still not enough."

— Eugene Delacroix

****

"If you do not breathe through writing, if you do not cry out in writing, or sing in writing, then don't write, because our culture has no use for it."

— Anais Nin

****

"The only reason for being a professional writer is that you can't help it."

— Leo Rosten

****

"Take a writer away from his typewriter and all you have left is the sickness that started him writing in the first place."

— Charles Bukowski

****

"Writing was like digging coal. I sweat blood. The spell is on me."

— Zane Grey

****

"If I don't write to empty my mind, I go mad."

— Lord Byron

****

"The work is a calling. It demands that type of obsession."

— John Pomfret

****

"Writing is a lifelong disease. Once contracted, the only prescription is to write constantly in whatever form to express your condition, in whatever construction to carry your words beyond you."

— J.R. Tompkins

****

"The moment I realize I just stayed up until five in the morning writing is that moment I know I am meant to be a writer."

— Anastasia Bolinder

****

"I have this desire to have this immaculate form of love that really doesn't exist, so my obsession goes on through life and I never find it and I end up miserable. But it makes me a better writer."

— Angel Haze

****

Chapter 22 – On Opportunity

"No great man ever complains of want of opportunities."

— Ralph Waldo Emerson

******

"A pessimist sees the difficulty in every opportunity; an optimist sees the opportunity in every difficulty."

— Winston Churchill

******

"We often miss opportunity because it's dressed in overalls and looks like work."

— Thomas Edison

******

"With everything that has happened to you, you can either feel sorry for yourself or treat what has happened as a gift. Everything is either an opportunity to grow or an obstacle to keep you from growing. You get to choose."

— Wayne Dyer

******

"You can't outwit fate by standing on the sidelines placing little side bets about the outcome of life. Either you wade in and risk everything you have to play the game or you don't play at all. And if you don't play you can't win."

— Judith McNaught

******

"It's the most satisfying occupation man has discovered yet, because you never can quite do it as well as you want to, so there's always something to wake up tomorrow morning to do."

— William Faulkner

****

"Failure is only the opportunity more intelligently to begin again."

— Henry Ford

****

"We will open the book. Its pages are blank. We are going to put words on them ourselves. The book is called Opportunity and its first chapter is New Year's Day."

— Edith Lovejoy Pierce

****

Chapter 23 – On Outlines and Structure

"Writing a novel is like heading out over the open sea in a small boat. It helps if you have a plan and a course laid out."

— John Gardner

****

"I'm a great believer in outlines."

— Tom Wolfe

****

"I'm a regular guy; I like well-defined outlines. I'm old-fashioned, bourgeois."

— Italo Calvino

****

"I'm a great planner, so before I ever write chapter 1, I work out what happens in every chapter and who the characters are. I usually spend a year on the outline."

— Ken Follett

****

"The most challenging and exciting aspect is the outline and formation of the plot points. This is the stage where the notion of the story begins to take shape, and I can see glimpses of what is to come."

— Tony DiTerlizzi

****

"The more work you put in on your outline and getting the skeleton of your story right, the easier the process is later."

— Drew Goddard

****

"I am a big outliner. For my adult book, 'The Visibles,' I did not outline, and it took me two years to write because I just didn't outline, and I had no path."

— Sara Shepard

****

"I'm a big fan of outlining. Here's the theory: If I outline, then I can see the mistakes I'm liable to make. They come out more clearly in the outline than they do in the pages."

— Cynthia Voigt

****

"Structure is important. Know your ending before you start writing. You wouldn't just get into your car and drive without knowing where you're going. Know your most important plot points. This does not mean things won't change, but you will never get stuck."

— Peter James

****

"If you do enough planning before you start to write, there's no way you can have writer's block. I do a complete chapter by chapter outline."

— R. L. Stine

****

"The outline is 95 percent of the book. Then I sit down and write, and that's the easy part."

— Jeffery Deaver

******

"I am a big proponent of writing a great outline. That way you can avoid hitting a roadblock. There is no worse feeling than writing yourself into a corner but if you've figured it all out in the outline then you won't have that problem."

— Michael Showalter

******

"I outline in some detail, but even after the outline is done I often get a new idea that is an improvement, so the outline is a living, breathing thing as well. I also re-outline when I'm two-thirds done, to be sure that there is an emotional payoff from all the plot lines and to be sure the story is as tight as it can be."

— Jeff Abbott

******

"I always work from an outline, so I know all the of the broad events and some of the finer details before I begin writing the book."

— Mercedes Lackey

******

"I have a number of writers I work with regularly. I write an outline for a book. The outlines are very specific about what each scene is supposed to accomplish."

— James Patterson

******

"I binge write, basically. I do a lot of prep, research, setup. I'll have a pretty detailed outline. Sort of like a beat outline. And then I'll add little notes and dialogue ideas, and I'll just create a 20-page document."

— Cary Fukunaga

****

"Putting pen to paper without first deciding the route and pace at which to scribe is like setting off on a bicycle without first checking the tyres."

— Fennel Hudson

****

"I'm one of those writers who tends to be really good at making outlines and sticking to them. I'm very good at doing that, but I don't like it. It sort of takes a lot of the fun out."

— Neil Gaiman

****

"Well, I outline fanatically. I am a long thinker and a slow writer, though I am trying to get faster."

— William Landay

****

"I like to make an outline on cards and then utterly ignore them."

— Margaret Stohl

****

"I am a writer who works from an outline. What I generally do when I build an outline is I find focal, important scenes, and I build them in my head and I don't write them yet, but I build towards them."

— Brandon Sanderson

****

"I always have a basic plot outline, but I like to leave some things to be decided while I write."

— J. K. Rowling

******

"I have notebooks and sketchbooks for ideas. I also have drawers full of envelopes covered in quick outlines, scenes or scraps of dialogue that I don't want to forget. I tend to grab whatever's to hand and just get the thing down before it's lost. It's not what you would call a streamlined system."

— Steven Hall

******

"Normally, I spend a week on the outline and take two weeks to write the book."

— R. L. Stine

******

"When I'm writing the first draft, I'm writing in a very slovenly way; anything to get the outline of the story on paper."

— Pat Barker

******

"My outlines can be 10-20 pages in length and focus primarily on the physical active plot over the emotional plot."

— Tony DiTerlizzi

******

"Outlining is like putting on training wheels. It gives me the courage to write, but we always go off the outline."

— Hallie Ephron

******

"For 'The Big Wander,' I probably had ten different outlines before I made myself start writing. I would sleep on each one, thinking it was wonderful, but I would always awake perceiving some flaw."

— Will Hobbs

****

"I write on big yellow legal pads – ideas in outline form when I'm doing stand-up and stuff. It's vivid that way. I can't type it into an iPad – I think that would put a filter into the process."

— Robin Williams

****

"I am not very good at sticking to outlines, and I double back all the time to revisit scenes and change things."

— Holly Black

****

"Don't write outlines; I hate outlines."

— George R. R. Martin

****

"I envy those writers who outline their novels, who know where they're going. But I find writing is a process of discovery."

— Jay McInerney

****

"Every book is like starting over again. I've written books every way possible – from using tight outlines to writing from the seat of my pants. Both ways work."

— Bruce Coville

****

"I think there are two types of writers, the architects and the gardeners. The architects plan everything ahead of time, like an architect building a house. They know how many rooms are going to be in the house, what kind of roof they're going to have, where the wires are going to run, what kind of plumbing there's going to be. They have the whole thing designed and blueprinted out before they even nail the first board up. The gardeners dig a hole, drop in a seed and water it. They kind of know what seed it is, they know if they planted a fantasy seed or mystery seed or whatever. But as the plant comes up and they water it, they don't know how many branches it's going to have, they find out as it grows. And I'm much more a gardener than an architect."

— George R.R. Martin

****

"I always have a rough outline, but I'm shocked at how little I actually follow it. Those characters keep doing things that I never expected. I think if I crept up to my keyboard and peeked, they'd be talking about things behind my back. Okay, that's a little paranoid and delusional... but just a little."

— Eric Walters

****

"I've often wished when I started a book I knew what was going to happen. I talked to writers who write 80-page outlines, and I'm just in awe of that."

— Charlaine Harris

****

"I routinely oscillate between exultation and despair. Maybe at the end of the day I feel pretty good about what I've written, but the next morning I see that it's crap. Then I start again – make a new outline, do some more research, try to rethink the whole question."

— Barbara Ehrenreich

****

"I start with a beat sheet, which is more of an abbreviated outline. It hits all the major plot points. From there, I move to note cards. But the most important part of my process is my inspiration board."

— Kami Garcia

****

"I start with an idea that is no more than a paragraph long, and expand it slowly into an outline. But I'm always surprised by the directions things take when I actually start writing."

— Barry Schwartz

****

"When writing, I uncage KAT: Keep Adding Tension. Even if I don't know where the story's going, petting the KAT keeps it purring."

— Don Roff

****

"The crafts of writing and carpentry are deceptively simple. The carpenter has to begin with a plan; the writer must begin with a thought. There must be at least the germ of an idea. Before the first board is nailed to the second board, or the first word connected to the second word, there has to be some clear notion of where we expect to be when we have finished nailing or writing."

— James J. Kilpatrick

****

Chapter 24 – On Perfectionism

"If you wait for perfect conditions, you will never get anything done."

— Paraphrased from Ecclesiastes 11:4

******

"Done is better than perfect if perfect ain't done."

— Eric Thomas

******

"Perfection is like chasing the horizon. Keep moving."

— Neil Gaiman

******

"Perfection is the enemy of creativity."

— Bangambiki Habyarimana

******

"Remember that fear always lurks behind perfectionism. Confronting your fears and allowing yourself the right to be human can, paradoxically, make you a far happier and more productive person."

— David M. Burns

******

"Perfectionism is self-abuse of the highest order."

— Anne Wilson Schaef

******

"At its root, perfectionism isn't really about a deep love of being meticulous. It's about fear. Fear of making a mistake. Fear of disappointing others. Fear of failure. Fear of success."

— Michael Law

****

"Good enough is good enough. Perfect will make you a big fat mess every time."

— Rebecca Wells

****

"You know, the whole thing about perfectionism. Perfectionism is very dangerous. Because, of course, if your fidelity to perfectionism is too high you never do anything. Because doing anything results in… it's actually kind of tragic because you sacrifice how gorgeous and perfect it is in your head for what it really is. And there were a couple of years where I really struggled with that."

— David Foster Wallace

****

"There is no perfection, only beautiful versions of brokenness."

— Shannon L. Alder

****

"But I am learning that perfection isn't what matters. In fact, it's the very thing that can destroy you if you let it."

— Emily Giffin

****

"Perfectionism is the voice of the oppressor, the enemy of the people. It will keep you cramped and insane your whole life, and it is the main obstacle between you and a shitty first draft. I think perfectionism is based on the obsessive belief that if you run carefully enough, hitting each stepping-stone just right, you won't have to die. The truth is that you will die anyway and that a lot of people who aren't even looking at their feet are going to do a whole lot better than you, and have a lot more fun while they're doing it."

— Anne Lamott

****

"Perfectionism doesn't believe in practice shots. It doesn't believe in improvement. Perfectionism has never heard that anything worth doing is worth doing badly – and that if we allow ourselves to do something badly we might in time become quite good at it. Perfectionism measures our beginner's work against the finished work of masters. Perfectionism thrives on comparison and competition. It doesn't know how to say, 'Good try,' or 'Job well done.' The critic does not believe in creative glee – or any glee at all, for that matter. No, perfectionism is a serious matter."

— Julia Cameron

****

"I am careful not to confuse excellence with perfection. Excellence I can reach for; perfection is God's business."

— Michael J. Fox

****

"Perfection is not attainable, but if we chase perfection we can catch excellence."

— Vince Lombardi

****

"The only characters I ever don't like are ones that leave no impression on me. And I don't write characters that leave no impression on me."

— Lauren DeStefano

Chapter 25 – On Perseverance

"I arise full of eagerness and energy, knowing well what achievement lies ahead of me."

— Zane Grey

****

"Success is most often achieved by those who don't know that failure is inevitable."

— Coco Chanel

****

"Always bear in mind that your own resolution to succeed is more important than any one thing."

— Abraham Lincoln

****

"It does not matter how slowly you go as long as you do not stop."

— Confucius

****

"If you are going through hell, keep going."

— Winston Churchill

****

"When you come to the end of your rope, tie a knot and hang on."

— Franklin D. Roosevelt

****

"Character consists of what you do on the third and fourth tries."

— James A. Michener

****

"The three great essentials to achieve anything worthwhile are, first, hard work; second, stick-to-itiveness; third, common sense."

— Thomas Edison

****

"The important thing in life is to have a great aim and a determination to attain it."

— Johann Wolfgang von Goethe

****

"Few things are impossible to diligence and skill. Great works are performed not by strength, but perseverance."

— Samuel Johnson

****

"You go on. You set one foot in front of the other, and if a thin voice cries out, somewhere behind you, you pretend not to hear, and keep going."

— Geraldine Brooks

****

"Courage and perseverance have a magical talisman, before which difficulties disappear and obstacles vanish into air."

— John Quincy Adams

****

"If you have a dream, don't just sit there. Gather courage to believe that you can succeed and leave no stone unturned to make it a reality."

— Roopleen

****

"At one time I thought the most important thing was talent. I think now that the young man or the young woman must possess or teach himself, training himself, in infinite patience, which is to try and try until it comes right."

— William Faulkner

****

"If you write one story, it may be bad; if you write a hundred, you have the odds in your favor."

— Edgar Rice Burroughs

****

"Reduce your plan to writing. The moment you complete this, you will have definitely given concrete form to the intangible desire."

— Napoleon Hill

****

"What is written without effort is in general read without pleasure."

— Samuel Johnson

****

"To make your life being a writer, it's an auto-slavery … you are both the slave and the task-master."

— Susan Sontag

****

"The difference between wanting to write and having written is one year of hard, relentless labour. It's a bridge you have to build all by yourself, all alone, all through the night, while the world goes about its business without giving a damn. The only way of making this perilous passage is by looking at it as a pilgrimage."

— Shatrujeet Nath

****

"Writing is like a lump of coal. Put it under enough pressure and polish it enough and you might just end up with a diamond. Otherwise, you can burn it to keep warm."

— A.J. Dalton

****

"You have to simply love writing, and you have to remind yourself often that you love it."

— Susan Orlean

****

"Be an unstoppable force. Write with an imaginary machete strapped to your thigh. This is not wishy-washy, polite stuff. It's who you want to be, your most powerful self. Write your books. Finish them, then make them better. Find the way. No one will make this dream come true for you but you."

— Laini Taylor

****

"Many of life's failures are people who did not realize how close they were to success when they gave up."

— Thomas Edison

****

"All makers must leave room for the acts of the spirit. But they have to work hard and carefully, and wait patiently, to deserve them."

— Ursula K. Le Guin

****

"Real courage is when you know you're licked before you begin, but you begin anyway and see it through no matter what."

— Harper Lee

****

"Don't let mental blocks control you. Set yourself free. Confront your fear and turn the mental blocks into building blocks."

— Roopleen

****

"The brick walls are there for a reason. The brick walls are not there to keep us out. The brick walls are there to give us a chance to show how badly we want something. Because the brick walls are there to stop the people who don't want it badly enough. They're there to stop the other people."

— Randy Pausch

****

"What is grander than a country and more valuable than gold? Strength of heart."

— Cornelius Elmore Addison

****

"A professional writer is an amateur who didn't quit."

— Richard Bach

****

"It's probably my job to tell you life isn't fair, but I figure you already know that. So instead, I'll tell you that hope is precious, and you're right not to give up."

— C.J. Redwine

****

"There are many ways of going forward, but only one way of standing still."

— Franklin D. Roosevelt

****

"A man of character finds a special attractiveness in difficulty, since it is only by coming to grips with difficulty that he can realize his potentialities."

— Charles de Gaulle

****

"The secret to becoming a writer is to write; write and keep on writing."

— Ken MacLeod

****

"If you fell down yesterday, stand up today."

— H.G. Wells

****

"Once you learn to quit, it becomes a habit."

— Vince Lombardi Jr.

****

"The thing with giving up is you never know. You never know whether you could have done the job. And I'm sick of not knowing about my life."

— Sophie Kinsella

****

"To create a market for your writing you have to be a consistent, professional, a continuing writer, not just a one-article or a one-story or a one-book man."

— Langston Hughes

****

"My belief of book writing is much the same as my belief as to shoemaking. The man who will work the hardest at it, and will work with the most honest purpose, will work the best."

— Anthony Trollope

****

"I've always found it best to have a routine. I go to my study at the same time every day and climb into my bay window. I may not be inspired every day, but on the days I am, I need to be in place to write. If I'm not particularly inspired, I'll revise or do research or correspondence."

— Diane Ackerman

****

"Because here's the secret: in the kingdom of God, as long as you're still fighting, you're winning. God doesn't hand out medals for performance. He hands out crowns for perseverance."

— Holley Gerth

****

"You know what I did after I wrote my first novel? I shut up and wrote twenty-three more."

— Michael Connelly

****

"Effort only fully releases its reward after a person refuses to quit."

— Napoleon Hill

****

"Real writers write. Period.

No, the muse does not come to visit every day. She's a lazy, precocious flirt. You cannot get into the habit of being 'in the mood' to write. No writer on Earth is in the mood to write every day, but the good ones do it anyway. They fight through their fatigue, their stress, their doubt, and they write. They get the words on the page. Period.

So stop waiting for your muse. Trust me, she sleeps around."

— Darynda Jones

****

Chapter 26 – On Plot

"To uncover the plot of your story, don't ask what should happen, but what should go wrong. To uncover the meaning of your story, don't ask what the theme is, but rather, what is discovered. Characters making choices to resolve tension – that's your plot. If your protagonist has no goal, makes no choices, has no struggle to overcome, you have no plot."

— Steven James

****

"When something goes wrong in your life just yell 'Plot Twist!' and move on."

— Molly Weis

****

"Remember: Plot is no more than footprints left in the snow after your characters have run by on their way to incredible destinations."

— Ray Bradbury

****

"Always mystify, torture, mislead and surprise the audience as much as possible."

— Don Roff

****

"Begin every story in the middle. The reader doesn't care how it begins, he wants to get on with it."

— Louis LAmour

****

"Be clear on every character's agenda in a scene, and the agendas in conflict. Before you write take just a moment to jot down what each character in the scene wants, even if (as Kurt Vonnegut once said) it is only a glass of water."

— James Scott Bell

****

"Character is plot, plot is character."

— F. Scott Fitzgerald

****

"I hate when people ask what a book is about. People who read for plot, people who suck out the story like the cream filling in an Oreo, should stick to comic strips and soap operas. Every book worth a damn is about emotions and love and death and pain. It's about words. It's about a man dealing with life. Okay?"

— J.R. Moehringer

****

"Story is honorable and trustworthy; plot is shifty, and best kept under house arrest."

— Stephen King

****

"Stories start in all sorts of places. Where they begin often tells the reader of what to expect as they progress. Castles often lead to dragons, country estates to deeds of deepest love (or of hate), and ambiguously presented settings usually lead to equally as ambiguous characters and plot, leaving a reader with an ambiguous feeling of disappointment. That's one of the worst kinds."

— Rebecca McKinsey

****

Chapter 27 – On Reading

"Read a thousand books, and your words will flow like a river."

— Lisa See

****

"If you don't have time to read, you don't have the time (or the tools) to write. Simple as that."

— Stephen King

****

"Read, read, read. Read everything – trash, classics, good and bad, and see how they do it. Just like a carpenter who works as an apprentice and studies the master. Read! You'll absorb it. Then write. If it's good, you'll find out. If it's not, throw it out of the window."

— William Faulkner

****

"What I do believe is that there is always a relationship between writing and reading, a constant interplay between the writer on the one hand and the reader on the other."

— Guillermo Cabrera Infante

****

"If you want to be a writer, you must do two things above all others: read a lot and write a lot...reading is the creative center of a writer's life...you cannot hope to sweep someone else away by the force of your writing until it has been done to you."

— Stephen King

****

"Learn as much by writing as by reading."

— Lord Acton

****

"I think we ought to read only the kind of books that wound or stab us. If the book we're reading doesn't wake us up with a blow to the head, what are we reading for? So that it will make us happy, as you write? Good Lord, we would be happy precisely if we had no books, and the kind of books that make us happy are the kind we could write ourselves if we had to. But we need books that affect us like a disaster, that grieve us deeply, like the death of someone we loved more than ourselves, like being banished into forests far from everyone, like a suicide. A book must be the axe for the frozen sea within us. That is my belief."

— Franz Kafka

****

"There are worse crimes than burning books. One of them is not reading them."

— Joseph Brodsky

****

"The greatest part of a writer's time is spent in reading in order to write. A man will turn over half a library to make a book."

— Samuel Johnson

****

"Reading makes a full man, meditation a profound man, discourse a clear man."

— Benjamin Franklin

****

"Tacitus did not write a most dangerous book. His readers made it so."

— Christopher B. Krebs

****

"The problem with our country isn't with books being banned but with people no longer reading. You don't have to burn books to destroy a culture. Just get people to stop reading them."

— Ray Bradbury

****

"Every once in a bestseller list, you come across a truly exceptional craftsman, a wordsmith so adept at cutting, shaping, and honing strings of words that you find yourself holding your breath while those words pass from page to eye to brain.

You know the feeling: you inhale, hold it, then slowly let it out, like one about to take down a bull moose with a Winchester .30-06.

You force your mind to the task, scope out the area, take penetrating aim, and . . . read.

But instead of dropping the quarry, you find you've become the hunted, the target. The projectile has somehow boomeranged and with its heat-sensing abilities (you have raised a sweat) darts straight towards you. Duck! And turn the page lest it drill between your eyes."

— Chila Woychik

****

"There are many rules of good writing, but the best way to find them is to be a good reader."

— Stephen E. Ambrose

****

"Words are the bones. Writing is the lungs. Reading is like breathing."

— T.L. Crain

******

"If we encounter a man of rare intellect, we should ask him what books he reads."

— Ralph Waldo Emerson

******

"Books are the quietest and most constant of friends; they are the most accessible and wisest of counselors, and the most patient of teachers."

— Charles William Eliot

******

"Some books should be tasted, some devoured, but only a few should be chewed and digested thoroughly."

— Francis Bacon

******

"Many people, myself among them, feel better at the mere sight of a book."

— Jane Smiley

******

Chapter 28 – On Rejection

"Rejection slips, or form letters, however tactfully phrased, are lacerations of the soul, if not quite inventions of the devil – but there is no way around them."

— Isaac Asimov

****

"Any reviewer who expresses rage and loathing for a novel is preposterous. He or she is like a person who has put on full armor and attacked a hot fudge sundae."

— Kurt Vonnegut

****

"Better to write for yourself and have no public, than to write for the public and have no self."

— Cyril Connolly

****

"Don't waste your energy trying to change opinions … Do your thing, and don't care if they like it."

— Tina Fey

****

"The first thing you have to learn when you go into the arts is to learn to cope with rejection. If you can't, you're dead."

— Warren Adler

****

"This manuscript of yours that has just come back from another editor is a precious package. Don't consider it rejected. Consider that you've addressed it '*to the editor who can appreciate my work*' and it has simply come back stamped '*Not at this address.*' Just keep looking for the right address."

— Barbara Kingsolver

****

"You have no responsibility to live up to what other people think you ought to accomplish. I have no responsibility to be like they expect me to be. It's their mistake, not my failing."

— Richard P. Feynman

****

". . . But then you will want to put that {publication} behind you right away. You will want to recover the obscurity you swim best through. You've got eternal youth there. You'll never be satisfied. If you get lucky, it will be a darkness so pure it will mirror not the 'self,' but the mysterious 'other.'"

— Louis B. Jones

****

"I got a rejection letter from an editor at HarperCollins, who included a report from his professional reader. This report shredded my first-born novel, laughed at my phrasing, twirled my lacy pretensions around and gobbed into the seething mosh pit of my stolen clichés. As I read the report, the world became very quiet and stopped rotating. What poisoned me was the fact that the report's criticisms were all absolutely true. The sound of my landlady digging in the garden got the world moving again. I slipped the letter into the trash…knowing I'd remember every word."

— David Mitchell

****

"I love my rejection slips. They show me I try."

— Sylvia Plath

******

"Every rejection is incremental payment on your dues that in some way will be translated back into your work."

— James Lee Burke

******

"I discovered that rejections are not altogether a bad thing. They teach a writer to rely on his own judgment and to say in his heart of hearts, 'To hell with you.'"

— Saul Bellow

******

"Rejection has value. It teaches us when our work or our skillset is not good enough and must be made better. This is a powerful revelation, like the burning UFO wheel seen by the prophet Ezekiel, or like the McRib sandwich shaped like the Virgin Mary seen by the prophet Steve Jenkins. Rejection refines us. Those who fall prey to its enervating soul-sucking tentacles are doomed. Those who persist past it are survivors. Best ask yourself the question: what kind of writer are you? The kind who survives? Or the kind who gets asphyxiated by the tentacles of woe?"

— Chuck Wendig

******

"As long as you look for someone else to validate who you are by seeking their approval, you are setting yourself up for disaster. You have to be whole and complete in yourself. No one can give you that. You have to know who you are – what others say is irrelevant."

— Nic Sheff

******

"Rejection sucks. It sucks every time, whether it's a big suck or a little suck. But it's part of the process. It's part of being a writer. It's a badge that says I'm serious about this, and I'm sending out my work."

— Allison K. Williams

****

"You have to know how to accept rejection and reject acceptance."

— Ray Bradbury

****

"The effects of rejection can either kill your muse or change your life."

— Jane Champagne

****

"We keep going back, stronger, not weaker, because we will not allow rejection to beat us down. It will only strengthen our resolve. To be successful there is no other way."

— Earl G. Graves

****

Chapter 29 – On Research

"If a writer knows enough about what he is writing about, he may omit things that he knows. The dignity of movement of an iceberg is due to only one ninth of it being above water."

— Ernest Hemingway

****

"If we knew what it was we were doing, it would not be called research, would it?"

— Albert Einstein

****

"Do research. Feed your talent. Research not only wins the war on cliché, it's the key to victory over fear and its cousin, depression."

— Robert McKee

****

"Get your facts first. Then you may distort them as you please."

— Mark Twain

****

"I have the right to interpretation as a dramatist. I research. It's my responsibility to find the research. It's my responsibility to digest it and do the best that I can with it. But at a certain point that responsibility will become an interpretation."

— Oliver Stone

****

"Never annoy an inspirational author or you will become the poison in her pen and the villain in every one of her books."

— Shannon L. Alder

Chapter 30 – On Retirement

"Only something extremely dire and disabling will ever stop a real writer from writing. Retirement is never an option."

— Warren Adler

****

"I'm 68 years old, and somebody asked if I'm retired. I told him, 'No, I'll still be writing long after I'm dead.'"

— Ron Brackin

****

"I didn't know that painters and writers retired. They're like soldiers – they just fade away."

— Lawrence Ferlinghetti

****

"I wonder what the retirement age is in the novel business. The day you die?"

— Yasunari Kawabata

****

"I often think about dogs when I think about work and retirement. There are many breeds of dog that just need to be working, and useful, or have a job of some kind, in order to be happy. Otherwise they are neurotically barking, scratching, or tearing up the sofa. A working dog needs to work. And I am a working dog."

— Martha Sherrill

****

"Retirement isn't a goal; it's a sentence."

— Ari Gold

****

"Once writing has become your major vice and greatest pleasure only death can stop it."

— Ernest Hemingway

****

Chapter 31 – On Self-Confidence

"I love my work but do not know how I write it."

— Zane Grey

****

"The writer must believe that what he is doing is the most important thing in the world. And he must hold to this illusion even when he knows it is not true."

— John Steinbeck

****

"People who repeatedly attack your confidence and self-esteem are quite aware of your potential, even if you are not."

— Wayne Gerard Trotman

****

"Believe you can and you're halfway there."

— Theodore Roosevelt

****

"You wouldn't worry so much about what others think of you if you realized how seldom they do."

— Eleanor Roosevelt

****

"Public opinion is a weak tyrant compared with our own private opinion."

— Henry David Thoreau

****

"And by the way, everything in life is writable about if you have the outgoing guts to do it, and the imagination to improvise. The worst enemy to creativity is self-doubt."

— Sylvia Plath

****

"If being an egomaniac means I believe in what I do and in my art or music, then in that respect you can call me that... I believe in what I do, and I'll say it."

— John Lennon

****

"Don't ask what the world needs. Ask what makes you come alive and go do it. Because what the world needs is people who have come alive."

— Howard Thurman

****

"Once we believe in ourselves, we can risk curiosity, wonder, spontaneous delight, or any experience that reveals the human spirit."

— E.E. Cummings

****

"A writer must teach himself that the basest of all things is to be afraid."

— William Faulkner

****

"All you need in this life is ignorance and confidence; then success is sure."

— Mark Twain

****

"I have great faith in fools – self-confidence my friends will call it."

— Edgar Allan Poe

****

"We either make ourselves miserable, or we make ourselves strong. The amount of work is the same."

— Carlos Castaneda

****

"Believe in yourself and there will come a day when others will have no choice but to believe with you."

— Cynthia Kersey

****

"You fail only if you stop writing."

— Ray Bradbury

****

"Fear defeats more people than any other one thing in the world."

— Ralph Waldo Emerson

****

"The moment you doubt whether you can fly, you cease for ever to be able to do it."

— J.M. Barrie

****

"Control Your Own Destiny or Someone Else Will."

— Jack Welch

****

"To guarantee success act as if it were impossible to fail."

— Dorothy Brande

****

"Let others determine your worth and you're already lost, because no one wants people worth more than themselves."

— Peter V. Brett

****

"You gain strength, courage, and confidence by every experience in which you really stop to look fear in the face."

— Eleanor Roosevelt

****

"The cave you fear holds the treasure you seek."

— Joseph Campbell

****

"Because one believes in oneself, one doesn't try to convince others. Because one is content with oneself, one doesn't need others' approval. Because one accepts oneself, the whole world accepts him or her."

— Lao Tzu

****

"You can never cross the ocean unless you have the courage to lose sight of the shore."

— Christopher Columbus

****

"When we do the best we can we never know what miracle is wrought in our life or in the life of another."

— Helen Keller

******

"The writer who loses his self-doubt, who gives way as he grows old to a sudden euphoria, to prolixity, should stop writing immediately: the time has come for him to lay aside his pen."

— Colette

******

"What the mind can conceive and believe, and the heart desire, you can achieve."

— Norman Vincent Peale

******

"The best writers I've read possess oodles of self-doubt, yet claw their way up with each work and remain humble. Boastful ones, not so much."

— Don Roff

******

"If writing seems hard, it's because it is hard. It's one of the hardest things people do."

— William Zinsser

Chapter 32 – On Show, Don't Tell

"Don't tell me the moon is shining; show me the glint of light on broken glass."

— Anton Chekhov

******

"Don't use adjectives which merely tell us how you want us to feel about the things you are describing. I mean, instead of telling us a thing was 'terrible,' describe it so that we'll be terrified. Don't say it was 'delightful;' make us say 'delightful' when we've read the description. You see, all those words (horrifying, wonderful, hideous, exquisite) are only like saying to your readers, 'Please, will you do my job for me?'"

— C.S. Lewis

******

"Show the readers everything, tell them nothing."

— Ernest Hemingway

******

"Storytellers don't show, they tell. I'm sticking with that."

— Ashly Lorenzana

******

"Good writing is supposed to evoke sensation in the reader – not the fact that it is raining, but the feeling of being rained upon."

— E.L. Doctorow

******

"Don't say the old lady screamed – bring her on and let her scream."

— Mark Twain

****

"You can tell your readers that two characters met and were instantly attracted to each other, or you could show the characters meeting, making eye contact, and checking each other out. He gulps, she bats her eyelashes, and readers get the picture."

— Melissa Donovan

****

"When modern readers pick up a book, they expect the story to play out like a film in their minds. They want to be fully immersed in the hero's experience just as they are when they turn on the TV. To see the scenes, smell the scents, and hear the sounds.

That is why *Show, Don't Tell* has become such a popular mantra among modern writers. It encourages writers to dive into that movie mindset, where things are seen and smelled and heard instead of simply written."

— Kristen Kieffer

****

Chapter 33 – On Solitude

"It's true that it's a solitary occupation, but you would be surprised at how much companionship a group of imaginary characters can offer once you get to know them."

— Anne Tyler

****

"Writing is utter solitude, the descent into the cold abyss of oneself."

— Franz Kafka

****

"Writing is something you do alone. It's a profession for introverts who want to tell you a story but don't want to make eye contact while doing it."

— John Green

****

"Without great solitude no serious work is possible."

— Picasso

****

"The writer's curse is that even in solitude, no matter its duration, he never grows lonely or bored."

— Criss Jami

****

"I want quiet thunder."

— Charles Bukowski

****

"Be alone, that is the secret of invention; be alone, that is where ideas are born."

— Nikola Tesla

****

"I need solitude for my writing: not 'like a hermit' – that wouldn't be enough – but like a dead man."

— Franz Kafka

****

"I lived in solitude in the country and I noticed how the monotony of a quiet life stimulates the creative mind."

— Albert Einstein

****

"Inside myself is a place where I live all alone, and that's where I renew my springs that never dry up."

— Pearl Buck

****

"I am alone here in my own mind. There is no map and there is no road."

— Anne Sexton

****

"Writing at its best, is a lonely life. Organizations for writers palliate the writer's loneliness, but I doubt if they improve his writing. He grows in public stature as he sheds his loneliness and often his work deteriorates. For he does his work alone and if he is a good enough writer he must face eternity, or the lack of it, each day."

— Ernest Hemingway

****

"In utter loneliness a writer tries to explain the inexplicable."

— John Steinbeck

******

"I can write best in the silence and solitude of the night, when everyone has retired."

— Zane Grey

******

"I am forever an advocate of books, both the reading of them and the writing. There is something sacred to me in that community. Because writing – and reading – is a solitary business. And it's good to know I'm not alone."

— Shannon Celebi

******

"My imagination functions much better when I don't have to speak to people."

— Patricia Highsmith

******

"It helps greatly in the avoidance of work to be in the company of others who are also waiting for the golden moment. The best place to write is by yourself because writing then becomes an escape from the terrible boredom of your own personality."

— John Kenneth Galbraith

******

"Prose is architecture, not interior decoration."

— Ernest Hemingway

Chapter 34 – On Story

"A successful story always offers its audience more than a simple resolution of events. A story offers a dramatic affirmation of human needs that are acted out to resolution and fulfillment. Even when that resolution and fulfillment are dark, the journey can still be vivid, potent and illuminating."

— Bill Johnson

****

"Begin your writing, fiction or article, where the action begins. This action can be internal (e.g., an important insight or personal decision) or external (e.g., a murder or calamity). Begin too early, you lose your reader. Begin too late, you lose your story."

— Walt Shiel

****

"Real suspense comes from moral dilemma and the courage to make and act upon choices. False suspense comes from accidental and meaningless occurrence of one damn thing after another."

— John Gardner

****

"You learn by writing short stories. Keep writing short stories. The money's in novels, but writing short stories keeps your writing lean and pointed."

— Larry Niven

****

"The important thing in writing is the capacity to astonish. Not shock – shock is a worn-out word – but astonish. The world has no grounds whatever for complacency. The Titanic couldn't sink but it did. Where you find smugness, you find something worth blasting. I want to blast it."

— Terry Southern

****

"Give the reader what they want, just not the way they expect it."

— William Goldman

****

"A scrupulous writer, in every sentence that he writes, will ask himself at least four questions, thus:

1. What am I trying to say?
2. What words will express it?
3. What image or idiom will make it clearer?
4. Is this image fresh enough to have an effect?

And he will probably ask himself two more.

1. Could I put it more shortly?
2. Have I said anything that is avoidably ugly?"

— George Orwell

****

"You can swap the message around, and whatever the particular norm is, or whatever the particular message is, when you put your pet-peeve message before story, odds are you are going to bore the shit out of your reader."

— Larry Correia

****

"Chapter one is where you reach out your hand to the reader and say, 'Come, let's have an adventure together.'"

— Tenaya Jayne

****

"Any idiot can write a long book. All it takes is patience and a willingness to keep pounding on the keys. A short book is a challenge. It's all about what you don't say. What you trust the reader to bring with them."

— Jason Sheehan

****

"Delayed gratification hints that something terrible is going to happen, and then delays the resolution. It's that interval between the promise of something awful and it actually happening, where suspense resides."

— Sandy Vaile

****

"...ugly interlopers threaten to choke off your story, depriving it of much-needed nutrition, sunlight and water. Identify and cut those weeds – the life-sucking adverbs, the shade-killing descriptions that don't move the story forward, the crowding passive voice sentences."

— Rob Bignell

****

"Screenplays are structure, and that's all they are. The quality of writing – which is crucial in almost every other form of literature – is not what makes a screenplay work. Structure isn't anything else but telling the story, starting as late as possible, starting each scene as late as possible. You don't want to begin with 'Once upon a time,' because the audience gets antsy."

— William Goldman

****

"On the whole, I think you should write biographies of those you admire and respect, and novels about human beings who you think are sadly mistaken."

— Penelope Fitzgerald

****

"There are a lot of ways for a novelist to create suspense, but also really only two: one a trick, one an art.

The trick is to keep a secret. Or many secrets, even. In Lee Child's books, Jack Reacher always has a big mystery to crack, but there are a series of smaller mysteries in the meantime, too, a new one appearing as soon as the last is resolved. J. K. Rowling is another master of this technique – Who gave Harry that Firebolt? How is Rita Skeeter getting her info?

The art, meanwhile, the thing that makes 'Pride and Prejudice' so superbly suspenseful, more suspenseful than the slickest spy novel, is to write stories in which characters must make decisions. 'Breaking Bad' kept a few secrets from its audience, but for the most part it was fantastically adept at forcing Walter and Jesse into choice, into action. The same is true of 'Freedom,' or 'My Brilliant Friend,' or 'Anna Karenina,' all novels that are hard to stop reading even when it seems as if it should be easy."

— Charles Finch

****

Chapter 35 – On Talent

"Talent is insignificant. I know a lot of talented ruins. Beyond talent lie all the usual words: discipline, love, luck, but most of all, endurance."

— James Baldwin

****

"Talent is God given. Be humble. Fame is man-given. Be grateful. Conceit is self-given. Be careful."

— John Wooden

****

"Your talent determines what you can do. Your motivation determines how much you are willing to do. Your attitude determines how well you do it."

— Lou Holtz

****

"The artist is nothing without the gift, but the gift is nothing without work."

— Émile Zola

****

"When talented people write badly, it's generally for one of two reasons: either they're blinded by an idea they feel compelled to prove or they're driven by an emotion they must express. When talented people write well it is generally for this reason: they're moved by a desire to touch the audience."

— Robert McKee

****

"Talent without working hard is nothing."

— Cristiano Ronaldo

****

"Writing a book is a blood sport. If it doesn't hurt when you're done, you're probably doing something wrong."

— Kevis Hendrickson

****

"However great a man's natural talent may be, the act of writing cannot be learned all at once."

— Jean-Jacques Rousseau

****

"Be a good steward of your gifts."

— Jane Kenyon

****

"There may be people who have more talent than you, but there's no excuse for anyone to work harder than you do – and I believe that."

— Derek Jeter

****

"I have no special talent. I am only passionately curious."

— Albert Einstein

****

"Talent is cheap; dedication is expensive. It will cost you your life."

— Irving Stone

****

"Everyone has talent. What's rare is the courage to follow it to the dark places where it leads."

— Erica Jong

******

"When I stand before God at the end of my life, I would hope that I would not have a single bit of talent left, and could say, I used everything you gave me."

— Erma Bombeck

******

"A winner is someone who recognizes his God-given talents, works his tail off to develop them into skills, and uses these skills to accomplish his goals."

— Larry Bird

******

"Mediocrity knows nothing higher than itself; but talent instantly recognizes genius."

— Arthur Conan Doyle

******

"Hide not your talents, they for use were made. What's a sundial in the shade?"

— Benjamin Franklin

******

"Talent is cheaper than table salt. What separates the talented individual from the successful one is a lot of hard work."

— Stephen King

******

"Your talent is God's gift to you. What you do with it is your gift back to God."

— Leo Buscaglia

****

"Talent without discipline is like an octopus on roller skates. There's plenty of movement, but you never know if it's going to be forward, backwards, or sideways."

— H. Jackson Brown, Jr.

****

"...talent means nothing, while experience, acquired in humility and with hard work, means everything."

— Patrick Süskind

****

"If you ever find that you're the most talented person in the room, you need to find another room."

— Austin Kleon

****

"Be led by your talent, not by your self-loathing; those other things you just have to manage."

— Russell Brand

****

"The most damning revelation you can make about yourself is that you do not know what is interesting and what is not."

— Kurt Vonnegut

****

"I want to say something so embarrassing about September that even the leaves start blushing and turning red."

— Jarod Kintz

****

"To be the kind of writer you want to be, you must first be the kind of thinker you want to be."

— Ayn Rand

****

"Use what talent you possess. The woods would be very silent if no bird sang except those that sang best."

— Henry Van Dyke

****

"Fine writers should split hairs together and sit side by side, like friendly apes, to pick the fleas from each other's fur."

— Logan Pearsall Smith

****

"Every artist was first an amateur."

— Ralph Waldo Emerson

****

"A good writer reveals beauty in the mundane and truth in tragedy. Words are a tool; a currency of the mind, and the best writers weave passages into our hearts that our bones remember."

— Maria Reeves

****

"Get through a draft as quickly as possible. Hard to know the shape of the thing until you have a draft. Literally, when I wrote the last page of my first draft of Lincoln's Melancholy I thought, Oh, shit, now I get the shape of this. But I had wasted years, literally years, writing and re-writing the first third to first half. The old writer's rule applies: Have the courage to write badly."

— Joshua Wolf Shenk

Chapter 36 – On Writer's Block

"Writer's block is just another name for fear."

— Jacob Nordby

******

"I have found repeatedly hitting my head with a mallet doesn't help at all, so I am open to suggestions."

— Steve Merrick

******

"There's no such thing as writer's block. That was invented by people in California who couldn't write."

— Terry Pratchett

******

"I just sit at my typewriter and curse a bit."

— P.G. Wodehouse

******

"If you are in difficulties with a book, try the element of surprise: attack it at an hour when it isn't expecting it."

— H.G. Wells

******

"Failure? I never encountered it. All I ever met were temporary setbacks."

— Dottie Walters

******

"You can't be blocked if you just keep on writing words. Any words. People who get 'blocked' make the mistake of thinking they have to write good words."

— Martha Grimes

****

"Discipline allows magic. To be a writer is to be the very best of assassins. You do not sit down and write every day to force the Muse to show up. You get into the habit of writing every day so that when she shows up, you have the maximum chance of catching her, bashing her on the head, and squeezing every last drop out of that bitch."

— Lili St. Crow

****

"I don't believe in writer's block. Do doctors have 'doctor's block?' Do plumbers have 'plumber's block?' No. We all have days when we don't feel like working, but why do writers turn that into something so damn special by giving it a faintly romantic name?"

— Larry Kahaner

****

"Unfortunately, many people suffer from BPS – Blank Page Syndrome. Let's face it: starting to write is scary. Seeing the cursor blinking at you on that bright white screen, realizing that you now have to come up with three or ten or twenty pages of text all on your own – it's enough to give anyone a major case of writer's block!"

— Stefanie Weisman

****

"Professional writers don't have muses; they have mortgages."

— Larry Kahaner

****

"You can't think yourself out of a writing block; you have to write yourself out of a thinking block."

— John Rogers

****

"I've often said that there's no such thing as writer's block; the problem is idea block. When I find myself frozen – whether I'm working on a brief passage in a novel or brainstorming about an entire book – it's usually because I'm trying to shoehorn an idea into the passage or story where it has no place."

— Jeffery Deaver

****

"Failing to write every day doesn't mean that you've given up, though a chapter a day keeps writer's block away!"

— David Batterson

****

"There are many advices on writing. The best I know is stop reading them and start writing."

— Bangambiki Habyarimana

****

"Do not wait to strike till the iron is hot; but make it hot by striking."

— William B. Sprague

****

"Why do I keep evading my work? Is it because I'm afraid of being confronted by my lack of abilities?"

— Candace Bushnell

****

"The best way is always to stop when you are going good and when you know what will happen next. If you do that every day . . . you will never be stuck. Always stop while you are going good and don't think about it or worry about it until you start to write the next day. That way your subconscious will work on it all the time. But if you think about it consciously or worry about it you will kill it and your brain will be tired before you start."

— Ernest Hemingway

****

"A problem with a piece of writing often clarifies itself if you go for a long walk."

— Helen Dunmore

****

"Don't waste time waiting for inspiration. Begin, and inspiration will find you."

— H. Jackson Brown Jr.

****

"Confront the page that taunts you with its whiteness. Face your enemy and fill it with words. You are bigger and stronger than a piece of paper."

— Fennel Hudson

****

"I think writer's block is simply the dread that you are going to write something horrible. But as a writer, I believe that if you sit down at the keys long enough, sooner or later something good will come out."

— Roy Blount, Jr.

****

"What is hell to a writer? Hell is being too busy to find the time to write or being unable to find the inspiration. Hell is suddenly finding the words but being away from your notebook or typewriter. Hell is when the verses slip through your fingers and they never return."

— R.M. Engelhardt

****

"Biting my truant pen, beating myself for spite: 'Fool!' said my muse to me, 'look in thy heart, and write.'"

— Philip Sidney

****

"The one ironclad rule is that I have to try. I have to walk into my writing room and pick up my pen every weekday morning."

— Anne Tyler

****

"There's no such thing as writer's block, so long as you've had plenty of time to think about what you want to write."

— Fennel Hudson

****

"I can fix a bad page. I can't fix a blank blank page."

— Nora Roberts

****

"Writer's block occurs when a writer has nothing to say. Unfortunately not all writers experience it."

— Ron Brackin

****

"I deal with writer's block by lowering my expectations. I think the trouble starts when you sit down to write and imagine that you will achieve something magical and magnificent – and when you don't, panic sets in. The solution is never to sit down and imagine that you will achieve something magical and magnificent. I write a little bit, almost every day, and if it results in two or three or (on a good day) four good paragraphs, I consider myself a lucky man. Never try to be the hare. All hail the tortoise."

— Malcolm Gladwell

****

"When you have made a thorough and reasonably long effort to understand a thing and still feel puzzled by it, stop. You will only hurt yourself by going on."

— Lewis Carroll

******

"Writer's block is my unconscious mind telling me that something I've just written is either unbelievable or unimportant to me, and I solve it by going back and reinventing some part of what I've already written so that when I write it again, it is believable and interesting to me. Then I can go on. Writer's block is never solved by forcing oneself to 'write through it,' because you haven't solved the problem that caused your unconscious mind to rebel against the story, so it still won't work – for you or for the reader."

— Orson Scott Card

******

"Planning to write is not writing. Outlining, researching, talking to people about what you're doing, none of that is writing. Writing is writing."

— E. L. Doctorow

******

"In my younger days dodging the draft, I somehow wound up in the Marine Corps. There's a myth that Marine training turns baby-faced recruits into bloodthirsty killers. Trust me, the Marine Corps is not that efficient. What it does teach, however, is a lot more useful.

The Marine Corps teaches you how to be miserable. This is invaluable for an artist.

Marines love to be miserable. Marines derive a perverse satisfaction in having colder chow, crappier equipment, and higher casualty rates than any outfit of dogfaces, swab jockeys, or flyboys, all of whom they despise. Why? Because these candy-asses don't know how to be miserable.

The artist committing himself to his calling has volunteered for hell, whether he knows it or not. He will be dining for the duration on a diet of isolation, rejection, self-doubt, despair, ridicule, contempt, and humiliation.

The artist must be like that Marine. He has to know how to be miserable. He has to love being miserable. He has to take pride in being more miserable than any soldier or swabbie or jet jockey. Because this is war, baby. And war is hell."

— Steven Pressfield

****

"Writer's Block is an imaginary mental illness invented by the 1% so they could control 99% of our creativity, and you can snap out of it on the count of 3 by just typing like a motherfucker."

— Andrea Balt

****

"Who is more to be pitied, a writer bound and gagged by policemen or one living in perfect freedom who has nothing more to say?"

— Kurt Vonnegut

****

"I learned never to empty the well of my writing, but always to stop when there was still something there in the deep part of the well, and let it refill at night from the springs that fed it."

— Ernest Hemingway

****

"Writing is 90 percent procrastination: reading magazines, eating cereal out of the box, watching infomercials. It's a matter of doing everything you can to avoid writing, until it is about four in the morning and you reach the point where you have to write."

— Paul Rudnick

****

"I haven't written in a week. It's like holding your breath under water. You feel an awful constriction and then the instinct to propel yourself."

— D.A. Botta

****

"You don't have to take it out on my typewrite ya' know. It's not the machine's fault that you can't write. It's a sin to do that to a good machine."

— Sam Shepard

****

"I haven't had trouble with writer's block. I think it's because my process involves writing very badly. My first drafts are filled with lurching, clichéd writing, outright flailing around. Writing that doesn't have a good voice or any voice. But then there will be good moments. It seems writer's block is often a dislike of writing badly and waiting for writing better to happen."

— Jennifer Egan

****

Chapter 37 – On Writing

"Know when it's time to put everything you've got on the page. Then, rip open a vein and do it!"

— Heather Burch

******

"A bird doesn't sing because it has an answer, it sings because it has a song."

— Maya Angelou

******

"It's the hardest thing in the world to write the second book. The first one was easy. We've all got a story to tell. But writing the second book, that's the difference between a professional and a not a professional."

— Robert Ludlum

******

"All the information you need can be given in dialogue."

— Elmore Leonard

******

"Write with the door closed, rewrite with the door open."

— Stephen King

******

"Write with the complete palette of emotions."

— Cindy Lambert

******

"Writing a novel is like driving a car at night. You can only see as far as your headlights, but you can make the whole trip that way."

— E. L. Doctorow

****

"Easy reading is damn hard writing."

— Nathaniel Hawthorne

****

"The first sentence can't be written until the final sentence is written."

— Joyce Carol Oates

****

"Here is a lesson in creative writing. First rule: do not use semicolons. They are transvestite hermaphrodites representing absolutely nothing. All they do is show you've been to college."

— Kurt Vonnegut

****

"Writing is easy. You only need to stare at a blank piece of paper until drops of blood form on your forehead."

— Gene Fowler

****

"When you're trying to create a career as a writer, a little delusional thinking goes a long way."

— Michael Lewis

****

"If you can tell stories, create characters, devise incidents, and have sincerity and passion, it doesn't matter a damn how you write."

— Somerset Maugham

****

"At its best, the sensation of writing is that of any unmerited grace. It is handed to you, but only if you look for it. You search, you break your heart, your back, your brain, and then – and only then – it is handed to you."

— Annie Dillard

****

"If you are using dialogue – say it aloud as you write it. Only then will it have the sound of speech."

— John Steinbeck

****

"If I ask you to think about something, you can decide not to. But if I make you feel something? Now I have your attention."

— Lisa Cron

****

"I recommend writing standing up from time to time. It's easier to dance when you finish writing."

— Diego Ramos

****

"Don't be a writer; be writing."

— William Faulkner

****

"So it is that a writer writes many books. In each book, he intended several urgent and vivid points, many of which he sacrificed as the books form hardened."

— Annie Dillard

****

"Any conversation between waking and working can be fatal. Before embarking on creative work or on a longish essay, I do need to know I am alone, and in the morning can go straight from my bed to my machine (after coffee) without speaking to anyone, and be there alone for at least two hours."

— Margaret Drabble

****

"I write 2,000 words a day when I write. It sometimes takes three hours, it sometimes takes five."

— Nicolas Sparks

****

"Most days, writing simply requires work-ethic, discipline, clarity, focus, time. Other days...it will demand absolutely everything of you."

— Christy Hall

****

Chapter 38 – On Writing Environments

"It's no secret that the best place to write, in my opinion, is in a café. You don't have to make your own coffee, you don't have to feel like you're in solitary confinement and if you have writer's block, you can get up and walk to the next café while giving your batteries time to recharge and brain time to think."

— J.K. Rowling

****

"I've learned that the creative life may or may not be the apex of human civilization, but either way it's not what I thought it was. It doesn't make you special and sparkly. You don't have to walk alone. You can work in an office – I've worked in offices for the past 15 years and written five novels while doing it. The creative life is forgiving: You can betray it all you want, again and again, and no matter how many times you do, it will always take you back."

— Lev Grossman

****

"We will need to find people who will provide a safe writing space for us, where criticism comes late and love and delight come early."

— L.L. Barkat

****

"The only environment the artist needs is whatever peace, whatever solitude, and whatever pleasure he can get at not too high a cost."

— William Faulkner

****

"I know some very great writers, writers you love who write beautifully and have made a great deal of money, and not one of them sits down routinely feeling wildly enthusiastic and confident. Not one of them writes elegant first drafts. All right, one of them does, but we do not like her very much."

– Anne Lamott

Chapter 39 – On Writing Every Day

"Just write every day of your life. Read intensely. Then see what happens. Most of my friends who are put on that diet have very pleasant careers."

— Ray Bradbury

****

"Exercise the writing muscle every day, even if it is only a letter, notes, a title list, a character sketch, a journal entry. Writers are like dancers, like athletes. Without that exercise, the muscles seize up."

— Jane Yolen

****

"We are what we repeatedly do. Excellence, therefore, is not an act but a habit."

— Aristotle

****

"This is how you do it: you sit down at the keyboard and you put one word after another until it's done. It's that easy, and that hard."

— Neil Gaiman

****

"If you want to be a writer, you have to write every day. You don't go to a well once but daily."

— Walter Mosley

****

"Volume depends precisely on the writer's having been able to sit in a room every day, year after year, alone."

— Susan Sontag

****

"Keep on beginning and failing. Each time you fail, start all over again, and you will grow stronger until you have accomplished a purpose…not the one you began with perhaps, but one you'll be glad to remember."

— Anne Sullivan Macy

****

"Don't wait for moods. You accomplish nothing if you do that. Your mind must know it has got to get down to work."

— Pearl S. Buck

****

"The one ironclad rule is that I have to try. I have to walk into my writing room and pick up my pen every weekday morning."

— Anne Tyler

****

"You can only write regularly if you're willing to write badly… Accept bad writing as a way of priming the pump, a warm-up exercise that allows you to write well."

— Jennifer Egan

****

"The desire to write grows with writing."

— Desiderius Erasmus

****

"10 Steps to Becoming a Better Writer:

1. Write.
2. Write more.
3. Write even more.
4. Write even more than that.
5. Write when you don't want to.
6. Write when you do.
7. Write when you have something to say.
8. Write when you don't.
9. Write every day.
10. Keep writing."

— Brian Clark

****

"If you don't make time for writing, writing won't make time for you."

— Sandra Elaine Scott

****

"Start writing, no matter what. The water does not flow until the tap is turned on."

— Louis LAmour

****

"My six words of advice to writers are: Read, read, read, write, write, write. Writing is a lonely job; you have to read and then you must sit down and write. There's no one there to tell you when to write, what to write, or how to write. I tell students if they are going to be writers they must sit down at a desk and write every day."

— Ernest J. Gaines

****

"Five minutes of writing a day is better than no minutes. Too many new writers think that unless they have plenty of time, it's not worth booting up the computer or sharpening that pencil. But think of it, instead, like practicing scales on the piano before tackling that Beethoven Concerto or like warming-up in the gym – the more you prepare for writing, the better shape you'll be in once you have time to really concentrate."

— Kate Mosse

****

"I never waited for my Irish Cream coffee to be the right temperature, with a storm happening outside and my fireplace crackling ... I wrote every day, at home, in the office, whether I felt like it or not, I just did it."

— Stephen J. Cannell

****

"Doing it all the time, whether or not we are in the mood, gives us ownership of our writing ability. It takes it out of the realm of conjuring where we stand on the rock of isolation, begging the winds for inspiration, and it makes it something as do-able as picking up a hammer and pounding a nail. Writing may be an art, but it is certainly a craft. It is a simple and workable thing that can be as steady and reliable as a chore – does that ruin the romance?"

— Julia Cameron

****

"There was a moment when I changed from an amateur to a professional. I assumed the burden of a profession, which is to write even when you don't want to, don't much like what you're writing, and aren't writing particularly well."

— Agatha Christie

****

"Sometimes you have to go on when you don't feel like it, and sometimes you're doing good work when it feels like all you're managing is to shovel shit from a sitting position."

— Stephen King

****

"Show up, show up, show up, and after a while the muse shows up, too."

— Isabel Allende

****

"So okay? There you are in your room with the shade down and the door shut and the plug pulled out of the base of the telephone. You've blown up your TV and committed yourself to a thousand words a day, come hell or high water. Now comes the big question: What are you going to write about? And the equally big answer: Anything you damn well want."

— Stephen King

****

"Bye-bye. Nice knowing you. But if you are waiting for that perfect idea to strike like lightning during a dust storm (I live in New Mexico), you could be waiting a long time. Ideas are everywhere. EVERYWHERE. I can't walk to the bathroom without being hit with another idea. It's what you DO with that idea that matters.

Here is your mantra: BITCHOK, BITCHOK, BITCHOK

Translation: Butt in chair, hands on keys. Just write. Every stinking day."

— Darynda Jones

****

"Imagine that you are dying. If you had a terminal disease would you finish this book? Why not? The thing that annoys this 10-weeks-to-live self is the thing that is wrong with the book. So change it. Stop arguing with yourself. Change it. See? Easy. And no one had to die."

— Anne Enright

One Last Thing!

Thank you for reading this book. If you enjoyed this book and found it useful I'd be grateful if you would post a brief review on Amazon. Every review helps this book find more of its readers.

http://christopherdiarmani.net/Review-Writing-Quotes-on-Amazon

Your support in the form of an honest review really does make a difference and helps this book find more readers. I also read every review personally so I can make my books even better.

I would also be grateful if you shared this book on social media.

If, for some reason, you did not like this book or didn't get what you expected out of it please tell me directly so I can use your constructive criticism to update the book to meet your expectations. You can contact me here:

http://ChristopherDiArmani.net/contact

Thank you so much for your support, feedback and your honest reviews on Amazon.

Sincerely,

Christopher di Armani
Author Extraordinare
http://ChristopherDiArmani.net/Books

Free Writing Timer for Authors

I do not believe in writer's block. I do, however, believe in writer's procrastination.

It's an affliction I suffer from each and every day. It's a plague on my productivity, as I am sure it is on yours.

One of the tools in my arsenal to combat procrastination is my Writing Timer. It's a simple little program (Windows only) that allows me to set an amount of time where I do nothing but write.

Of course I wrote the program as part of my own procrastination from writing. Ironic, right?

The concept is simple. Open the timer. Set it for 5, 10, 15, 20 or 30 minutes.

Click Start. Then write.

It doesn't matter what you write. Just write like you're possessed by demons. Or chased by them. Whatever works.

Whenever you know you ought to be writing but are doing everything *except* writing, admit defeat at the hands of writer's procrastination and start the timer.

Then write.

It just works.

To get your free copy of my writing timer just visit the link below.

http://christopherdiarmani.net/Free-Writing-Timer

****

About Christopher di Armani
"Author Extraordinaire"

The hardest writing for any author, I suspect, is writing about themselves.

It sure is for me. I can write the most personal quirks and embarrassing situations for any character in my fiction. Writing about myself is… uncomfortable.

I'm not one for the spotlight. I like the shadows. I'm most comfortable there. Most writers are.

Writing is my passion and I'm my happiest when I'm pounding out a story.

Like many writers I am an avid reader. My earliest memories are of Zane Grey westerns. I devoured them like candy. His strong male characters, no matter their personal flaws, did the right thing when it counted. That is what drew me to his books. I imagine I learned a lot of my own moral code from the characters Zane Grey created.

Like many writers I am an introvert. Do not allow the protestations of past co-workers convince you otherwise. They see what I want them to see – the social face that allows me to function out in the world.

Every writer has one. It's how we survive until we make our way back to the safety and security of our writing room.

I am a good writer.

That's not arrogance speaking. That's a fact substantiated by the money folks pay me to write. Bad writers don't get paid.

I didn't start off a good writer though. My first novel, written when I was 16, is proof of that. It's about teenage gangs in high school, about bad choices and worse friends. I wrote it as an assignment for English class.

My teacher took pity on me and commended me for its length and ambition with a C Plus. Notice he did not say *talent*.

The book is horrible. Really. I stumbled across it a few years ago and attempted to read it. By the end of the first page I wanted to vomit. It's trash. I accept that.

I started writing young and wrote anything that struck my fancy. Some published, most wasn't. I wrote letters to the editor, newspaper articles, short stories, poetry, novellas, books, short films and feature-length screenplays.

Major newspapers, both print and digital, published me as time passed and talent increased.

Then I edited a national magazine for a firearms advocacy group for two years. That's where I learned first-hand just how hard we writers make it on our editors. During my tenure as magazine editor I learned how to edit *anything* into readable form. Why? I had to meet deadline.

That's a lesson that serves me well to this day.

I'm also a huge horror movie fan. I love vampires (*not the ones that sparkle*), werewolves and scary guys like Hannibal Lector.

My interests vary as do my forms and genres of writing. I love writing current events commentary. That love turned into a book on the RCMP's ongoing issues as well as a book on Canada's 23rd Prime Minister, Justin Trudeau.

I've written a vampire movie and a series of two serial killer movies and I'm turning all three scripts into novels. I just finished the first draft of the novel based on the vampire script. When I finish that I'll turn the two serial killer movies into novels and add the third and final installment to that series.

Along the way I'm sure I will write other odd things, too. Like most writers I too have more ideas than I have time to write.

That's the joy of the creative mind, isn't it?

I also love art but cannot draw to save my life. Hold a gun to my head and say "draw or die" and I'll make my peace with God while awaiting your bullet. The good Lord gave me many talents but drawing is not one of them.

That's why I love Poser, a 3D image creation and animation program. It allows me to fulfill my artistic desires despite my complete lack of artistic ability.

As a writer I love Poser. I use it to create character reference images for my characters. I have a concrete vision of who my characters are, what they look like, what they wear, how they hold themselves, etc. Poser gives me the power to translate the vision in my head onto my computer screen. I print them out, pin them to the wall and ponder them when I need inspiration.

If you've managed to reach the end of this wandering diatribe I both thank you for your patience and commend you for your perseverance. There's nothing worse than reading about someone droning on about themselves!

Since you're still here I'd love to keep you updated about what I'm writing next. Just visit my website below.

http://ChristopherDiArmani.net

Until our paths cross again…

Christopher di Armani
Author Extraordinaire
http://ChristopherDiArmani.net/Books

Books by Christopher di Armani

The Simple 3-Step Secret to Slaughter Writer's Block And Vanquish it Forever

We writers are fickle beings. Or at least we can be. Our vivid and often prolific imaginations run wild given the slightest prodding and we lose sight of reality far more easily than the average person.

That's not a bad thing. It's actually a huge benefit given our chosen career. But that fickle imagination can also trap us with lies.

The biggest lie of all is that we can't write. We can write. We can always write. Sometimes we just need to be reminded of that simple fact and my Simple 3-Step Secret is just the ticket when Writer's Block has you under its thumb.

****

TOP SECRET – Inspiration, Motivation and Encouragement – 701 Essential Quotes for Writers

This book is a compilation of 701 quotes covering 39 aspects of writing and the writing life. Within its pages you will discover quotes to make you laugh and bring a tear to your eye. Some will be as familiar as an old friend, others will be brand new.

The common theme is this: we writers are the same no matter what we write about and we learn from one another. It's meant as a resource for writers in need of inspiration or encouragement late at night or early in the morning. It's meant to cheer you up as well as make you think. Above all it's meant to build a deep desire to write inside you.

Justin Trudeau – 47 Character-Revealing Quotes from Canada's 23rd Prime Minister and What They Mean for You

On October 19, 2015 Canadians elected their 23rd Prime Minister based on good looks, nice hair and a famous name. They voted for style over substance.

Our 23rd Prime Minister's entire leadership experience consisted of teaching snowboarding lessons and high school drama. His management experience consisted of administering his trust fund and his ego.

Not a single thought was given to what he stood for, what his party stood for, or what he would actually do once elected to the highest office in the land.

That bothered me. That bothered me so much I began to research his much-publicized missteps and that in turn revealed a disturbing pattern within Trudeau's numerous faux pas.

That pattern is the focus of this book.

****

RCMP Thugs, Thieves and Liars: The Appalling Lack of Accountability in Canada's National Police Force

The RCMP's deep, plentiful and systemic problems lend to much spilled ink by writers like me. They make the RCMP an easy target for commentators who, for one reason or another, dislike one or more of the following: cops, the RCMP, thugs in uniform, thieves in uniform, serial sexual abusers, bullies and an internal system of discipline that is a rude joke.

Me, I don't dislike cops in general. In fact I cannot think of a single interaction with a uniformed RCMP member that has left a bad feeling in my mouth. The RCMP's lack of accountability, however, is another story entirely.